MW00462947

better
GOOD
than
LUCKY

How Savvy Investors Create Fortune
with the Risk-Reward Ratio

better
GOOD
than
LUCKY

How Savvy Investors Create Fortune
with the Risk-Reward Ratio

BY CHARLES ROTBLUT, CFA

One Peregrine Way, Cedar Falls, Iowa 50613
www.w-apublishing.com | www.traderspress.com

Published by W&A Publishing, Cedar Falls, Iowa www.w-apublishing.com.

Library of Congress Control Number: 2010929234
ISBN: 978-1-934354-14-8
ISBN-10: 1-934354-14-7
Printed in the United States of America
10 9 8 7 6 5 4 3 2 1

For my beautiful wife Marni, who has patiently allowed me to chase my dreams, and for my parents, George and Micheline, and my inlaws, Les and Lila, who deserve gratitude for everything they have given us.

I wish to thank John Jagerson, Sheraz Mian, Jason Napodano, and Steve Reitmeister for their help in bringing this book to fruition.

Contents

Foreword

Many volumes of great investment literature have been written in the last 100 years. The problem is the average investor does not have time to read all of this literature, much less grasp the key concepts.

This book solves the problem by explaining key investing concepts in easy-to-understand language.

The book is based on four primary concepts:

- Diversification
- Strong business model
- Good financials
- Attractive valuation

These four concepts, used by professionals for years, reflect Harry Markowitz's theories on portfolio construction, Philip Fisher's writings on business models, and Benjamin Graham's focus on financial strength and value.

Harry Markowitz revolutionized portfolio management and was awarded a Nobel Prize for his efforts. Fisher and Graham are said to have influenced Warren Buffett. Also incorporated are strategies from Len Zacks (earnings surprises and earnings estimate revisions), John Bogle (controlling investment expenses), and Burton Malkiel (the randomness of stock market returns).

This book does more than incorporate past literature; it reflects my many years of experience in the financial services industry. I led the development of the Zacks Method for Investing, a stock selection methodology used to manage the model portfolios on *Zacks.com*, which has significantly outperformed the S&P 500. I understand what makes a stock a good value and what does not.

Equally important to the individual investor, this book explains how to analyze a stock like a professional. I have created a reference guide, enabling investors to get the information they need when they need it. This goes deeper than a step-by-step process to provide valuable information on:

- The Investment Community and Your Portfolio
- Corporate Analysis
- Valuation
- Creating Your Own Luck

Sincerely,
Charles Rotblut, CFA

Introduction:
The Risk-Reward Ratio

Smart investors create their own "luck."

In reality, this concept holds true because smart investors position themselves to profit. They maintain a constant exposure to the market and thus profit when the markets make large, unexpected gains. They analyze each investment before buying it and then continue to analyze it afterward. They make sure they understand the potential risks and keep an eye out for those risks. They never fall in love with a stock, but view it as a means to an end—a vehicle for creating wealth. Most importantly, they avoid risky investments. In other words, smart investors use the Risk-Reward Ratio to their advantage.

What is the Risk-Reward Ratio? It is a measure of the probability a stock will decrease in price ("risk") versus the probability the stock will increase in price ("reward"). The lower the amount of risk and the greater potential for reward, the higher the probability you will make money.

Limiting risk is about avoiding stocks likely to decrease in price. Often these are companies trading at excessive valuations. You have heard about many of these companies; their stock is the hot stock of the day and everybody is buying shares because investors are convinced the share price is going to keep rising. Business will only get better. The fact that the share price is no longer being tied to the company's projected growth rate or the presence of competitors eager to cut into the company's market share are often ignored; such concerns are crazy talk. Yet when the company finally stumbles or fails to exceed expectations by as much as everyone thought, shares of the stock become a hot potato. Everyone cannot wait to sell the stock and, consequently, the share price tumbles.

Maximizing reward is about identifying the bargain stocks. These are companies with strong management, good business models, and solid financial strength. They have a history of profitability and systems in place to ensure profits grow. Equally important, these are stocks with relatively low valuations. Their prices suggest the broader market has yet to take notice of the overall appeal. When such stocks do get noticed, they benefit from both sustained profit growth and increased demand from other interested investors. This is a powerful combination that causes the share price to move higher.

Successful investors adhere to the Risk-Reward Ratio, whether consciously or unconsciously. They spend time analyzing a company, figuring out what makes it tick and why it should (or should not) be successful. They look for potential weaknesses and assess whether those weaknesses outweigh the positives. They analyze the price to determine if the stock is a compelling bargain and if there is justification for the price to appreciate further. They understand the financial health of the company and they know what would cause them to sell the stock before they ever buy it.

People often call successful investors bold or courageous. These investors are lauded for taking large bets ahead of or against current trends. A more appropriate term might be *smart*. While successful investors are aware of current fads, they are more concerned with whether a stock offers a compelling Risk-Reward Ratio than what the broader investment community is doing. Sometimes successful investors purchase stocks considered to be out of favor. Sometimes the stocks are in popular sectors. It does not matter. What does matter is at prevailing prices, the stocks are bargains.

This book will teach you how to find those bargains.

INVESTMENT PHILOSOPHY

When I set out to write this book, a friend asked what I could add to the volumes of material already written. Even a brief visit to the business section of a public library reveals thousands of pages about investing and trading. A number of books are good, but several are written for the purpose of enriching their authors. Those investors who chose to follow the advice in those books found that their investment losses greatly exceeded the cost of the book. But some books and studies stand apart. Within their pages are thoughts and revelations influencing some of the greatest investors of our time. Most investors have never read these books and studies, much less benefited from their advice.

The reason for writing this book is to provide investors with a single book that is easy to read and based on sound investment theories and thought. If I have done my job successfully, you will gain the benefit of time-tested principles and my professional experience.

This book contains four underlying themes: a strong business model, good financials, an attractive valuation, and diversification. These themes are not sound bites – they are the cornerstones of a good investment philosophy.

Several surveys, conducted by companies I have worked for, have shown most individual investors lack a philosophy. This is akin to driving across the country without a map. You might eventually find your way to Seattle from Jacksonville, but more likely you would have wasted more time and energy than if you had a plan for making the trip successful. Investing without a philosophy is no different. You may make money in the end, but not as much as you could have and with more volatility than you would have encountered otherwise. What I see is investors who want to make money now, but are afraid of losing money, or investors who describe themselves as value investors, but invest in companies in vogue right now.

An investment philosophy prevents this from happening. Rather than succumbing to the whims of the market, you are able to remain focused on making money. You know how you want to invest your money and seek out those investments best matching your philosophy. Your own philosophy might be different from your neighbor's, but the cornerstones should always remain the same: diversification, a strong business model, good financials, and an attractive valuation. Base your philosophy around these four cornerstones and you will make money.

Diversification – Any stock, any industry and any asset class can fall out of favor at any time. Therefore, it is important to spread your portfolio over a number of investments. You should own multiple stocks in different industries and own assets outside of stocks (e.g. bonds, real estate, etc.). The advantage to diversification is not limited to safety; it is also directly related to performance. A properly diversified portfolio will generate a higher level of return relative to the level of risk taken. In other words, diversification allows you to profit more and protect your money better – and that is getting the Risk-Reward Ratio to work in your favor. Diversification is discussed in Chapter 2.

Business Model – A business model is what a company does to make money. Take for instance a hot dog stand. The vendor makes money by selling hot dogs. If he knows what he is doing, he has placed his stand in a well-trafficked area where people are in the mood to eat hot dogs. Competitive hot dog stands should be few in number. The vendors should be supplying good quality meats, buns, and condiments at reasonable prices. Obviously, the business model for a corporation is more complex than a hot dog stand, but the underlying basis for success remains the same: get customers what they want at a price profitable to the company. Business models are discussed in Chapter 4.

Good Financials – Financial statements are the key to analyzing any company and yet are the most overlooked piece of information. Even a cursory glance can reveal if the company is generating value for its shareholders or going through cash at a dangerously high pace. More time spent looking over the financial statements will show whether the company is paying its bills, managing its inventory, keeping expenses under control, and not excessively issuing stock (thereby diluting the value of shareholder's holdings). The more financially sound a company is, the more shareholders stand to profit. The weaker a company's financial status is, the more likely the company will create anxiety for its shareholders. Put another way, would you prefer to lend money to a person with a good credit history and a good career or someone on the verge of bankruptcy and at risk of being fired? Financial statements are discussed in chapters 5-7.

Attractive Valuation – Valuation is the most important determinant of whether a stock's returns will be greater or less than those of the broader markets over the long-term. Numerous studies have shown an inverse relationship between a stock's valuation and its performance. The lower a stock's valuation is, the better it will perform. A low valuation suggests investors are not recognizing a company's potential to generate profits in the future. A high valuation suggests investors are optimistic about a company's prospects and are pricing the stock accordingly.

A company whose price is based on a bright outlook has more opportunity to disappoint, whereas a company not expected to perform well has more opportunity to surprise investors. (Under-promising and over-delivering have always been a good recipe for success in the financial markets.) Not all stocks with a low valuation are good buys; some stocks deserve to trade at low valuations because they will not generate good profits. Throughout this book, I will show you how to spot the real bargains. The topic of valuation is discussed in chapters 8-9.

In summary, a stock is a candidate for purchase if the company has a good business model and strong financials, the valuation is low and the investment maintains diversification in your portfolio. Following these four cornerstones will improve your chances of making money and reduce your risk of losing money.

GROWTH INVESTING

Some of you will notice the word "growth" is nowhere to be found in the discussion of cornerstones. This is intentional.

Growth occurs when a company is properly run. A good business model enables earnings growth and good financials fund the growth. Conversely, growth does not create a good business model or strong financials. A company could be at the right place at the right time, but be unable to sustain itself as an ongoing entity once conditions change. This occurred during the technology bubble of the 1990s when many dot-com companies showed strong growth before plunging in value and eventually disappearing. I am not anti-growth. It is important for a company to develop new streams of revenues and find ways to increase profits. The problem with growth investing lies with expectations. The more investors expect a company to continue delivering strong growth, the greater the chance it will disappoint.

Stock performance is related to expectations – perform better than investors expect and the stock price will rise. Perform worse than investors expect and the stock price will decline. Since no one has successfully mastered the art of forecasting, the best an investor can do is to find companies with a probability of earnings growth being underestimated by the broader markets.

I realize many readers have been indoctrinated to equate growth with profitable returns. The lessons taught on the following pages apply equally to aggressive growth strategies and conservative value strategies. Good companies create their own opportunities for growth. You should invest in well-managed companies with strong financials, which are trading at a discount relative to their prospects, and spread your portfolio allocation among different stocks in different industries. Remember, the higher the valuation is, the smaller the margin of error. There can be big rewards for investing in a company with explosive growth, but the risks are often greater.

During any period of strong economic growth, numerous pundits will proclaim, "it is different this time." Shortly thereafter, this motto shifts to a rationale for ignoring valuations and focusing on growth. The justification for a new way of thinking is because conditions have changed enough to fuel exponential growth for an extended period of time.

This is what occurred during the technology bubble of the late 1990s. Rapid growth of the Internet was credited with fundamentally changing business, economic, and market dynamics. Some observers went so far as to say retail chains operating physical stores would be forced out of business by the newer, upstart e-commerce companies. What occurred, though, is many dot-com companies floundered or went bankrupt, while established retail chains, with their brick-and-mortar stores, grew stronger. The older and financially stable companies adapted and used their reputation to capture consumers. Furthermore, many consumers learned to combine Internet research with physical shopping as opposed to doing everything on their PCs.

Stock prices reacted accordingly. During the Internet bubble, dot-com companies gave investors substantial short-term profits and the illusion that stellar revenue growth would turn into large profits. Valuations were ignored as hype replaced rationality. Starting around March 2000, the punch bowl started running low and the music stopped playing. Internet stars started running low on cash and found themselves unable to raise more. Lofty valuations turned into plunging stock prices, wrecking havoc in multiple portfolios. Investors ran for the sidelines and value managers who were fired during the bubble suddenly regained their appeal.

It took nearly 10 years after the bubble for the e-commerce poster child *Amazon.com* to rebound to the highs it reached in January 2000. *Pets.com* has been gone for a long time. Many technology stocks – the companies that were supposed to be supplying the pans to this gold rush, such as PMC-Sierra—trade at less than 10% of their bubble highs.

The pundits who proclaimed it is different this time were wrong. It might be easy to say the pundits overlooked something in their forecasts or were too early in their calls, but both would be nothing more than a convenient excuse. What occurred was history repeating itself.

In the late 1920s, valuation models used for years were thrown out the window. Growth was projected to remain strong for years to come as pundits declared a new era had begun. Lay people who had never invested a dollar were suddenly talking about stocks. Ticker tapes began appearing in unusual places like beauty salons, elevator attendants provided stock tips and business school attendance swelled. Investing on margin was not only easy to do, but encouraged. Meanwhile, those who dared to question if equity markets could maintain their strength were ignored, if not chastised.

In the autumn of 1929, equity markets started to wobble. Rather than view it for what it was – a shot across the deck – investors viewed it as a buying opportunity. Then the markets crashed in October of that year. Large fortunes were lost overnight and smaller, personal accounts vanished into the ether. Up-and-coming companies suddenly slashed their workforces in a drastic effort to stay open. The Dow lost 12% in one day and proceeded to drop with a cumulative three-year loss of nearly 90%. Following this crash, Ben Graham and David Dodd published what is still considered to be one of the best investing books ever written, *Securities Analysis*. Its concept? Buy fundamentally sound companies trading at discount valuations—advice completely ignored a few years before by investors convinced potential growth mattered more than valuation.

One reason why stock prices rose too much in the 1920s and the 1990s— as well as other periods—was that forecasts were given more weight than valuations. Investors believed several companies could maintain exceptional growth rates for years to come. Worse yet, they believed if they did not buy shares in a fast-growing company, the stock would be much more expensive in the future, costing them a great amount in lost potential profits. Besides, their friends, coworkers, and relatives were getting rich, so why should they be grinches and miss out on the party? Fear of being left behind is a powerful force and has caused many an investor to make irrational decisions.

The inherent problem with manias is forecasts are usually wrong. Predicting the state of the economy and what a company will earn 12 months from now is difficult. Projecting a company's profits 24 months from now with accuracy is nothing more than an educated guess. Predicting what a company will earn three to five years from now, a statistic some growth investors use to justify their investment decisions, is impossible. To make matters worse, numerous surveys have shown an optimistic bias among brokerage analysts, meaning they underestimate the possibility of disappointments in the future. Also when things are going well, most people tend to be overly optimistic about their prospects.

Placing an emphasis on valuation provides a margin of safety against making mistakes. A low valuation suggests investors are not optimistic about the future (or apathetic about the company). Conversely, a high valuation suggests investors expect great things from the company. The equity markets reward companies exceeding expectations and punish companies that disappoint. The greater the optimism priced into a stock, the greater the opportunity for disappointment. Stocks with low valuations, on the other hand, have a greater opportunity to exceed expectations, because investors are not expecting good news. Buy low, sell high.

INVESTING VERSUS TRADING

The old adage of buy low, sell high is used without much thought. Buy low, sell high means buying a stock (or any security) at a discounted price and selling it at as great a profit as possible. It makes no difference as to how long a stock is held. For the purposes of this book, buying low means acquiring stocks at prices not adequately reflecting the company's prospects. Selling high means closing out your position when you can no longer justify holding onto the security. For an investor who has conducted adequate research, the period of time between buying low and selling high can be considerable and the profits impressive.

The period of time a stock is held defines the difference between investing and trading. Investors take an ownership stake in the company.

They understand the business, know how the company should be priced and follow the company's business. Most importantly, they buy the stock intending to hold onto the position for an extended period. Traders seek a short-term profit. They are not concerned with a stock's valuation or a company's business. Their primary concern is the price and whether it will be higher over the next few days or weeks. Traders have no intention of holding onto the stock for more than a short period. Either they make a quick profit or they do not. Trading is speculation, investing is ownership. Trading is the risky pursuit of profits; investing seeks to minimize risk and maximize gain.

There is nothing wrong with trading and many people have made considerable profits by speculating on short-term price movements, but trading entails high risk. For every person who has profited from trading, there are many more who have lost significant amounts of money. Part of the problem is emotional; people do not want to admit they are wrong and, as a result, are hesitant to take a loss. Trading strategies involve making correct assumptions about short-term movements in price; when these price movements do not occur, the stock must be sold immediately.

Another problem is overconfidence. Successful traders make speculating seem easy. The reality is trading is difficult and contains little room for error. Trading the wrong stocks also adds to the potential for failure. Trading involves flexibility—what was in play yesterday may no longer be an attractive trade today. Traders must constantly scan the market to find out which stock is worth speculating. The most common problem is that trades become investments when short-term profits are not realized. Rather than take a small loss when the stock declines in price, people hold onto the position, hoping the stock will bounce back. Trading is short-term speculation; when the price does not immediately rise, the position must be sold.

Investing, on the other hand, provides room for error. Investors are not concerned with the short-term fluctuations of the markets because they are looking for stocks priced at unreasonably low valuations. Not purchasing the stock at the best trading is okay; what matters is what the stock's price will be six, 12 or 60 months from now. When analysis is properly done before the stock is purchased, the long-term gains can be considerable.

HOW THIS BOOK IS ORGANIZED

In writing this book my intention was to keep it short. I sought to cover the key factors involving stock investing (including portfolio management, business model analysis, financial statement analysis, and valuation) in as few pages as possible. I wanted this book to be a reference you could frequently consult.

In accomplishing this, I grouped the chapters into four sections: The Investment Community and Your Portfolio, Corporate Analysis, Valuation, and Creating Your Own Luck. Each section and chapter builds on the previous one. Outside of a few references, if you start with the valuation section and work your way toward the chapters on portfolio management, this book will still make sense. Read it in the order that makes the best sense to you.

The Investment Community and Your Portfolio

Everyone likes to use the term, "the markets," but what are the markets? More importantly, how do you use the markets most effectively to make money? Chapters 1, 2, and 3 answer these questions. Chapter 1 explains the various sources to obtain investment advice, including brokerage analysts, financial advisors, the media, and even blogs. Once you understand the role of each player, you will be able to make better decisions about the information provided. Chapter 2 delves into the academia world and explains one of the best known theories regarding portfolio management: Modern Portfolio Theory. Understanding this theory will help you build a portfolio that minimizes risk and expenses, while maximizing returns. Chapter 3 discusses another important part of portfolio management—psychology. You will learn strategies to make objective decisions and assess overall market sentiment.

Corporate Analysis

Minimizing risk and maximizing reward is based on having a thorough understanding of how a company makes money and manages its assets. These four chapters will show you how to analyze a business like a pro. Chapter 4 discusses how to a look at a company's business model and determine whether it will be successful. Chapters 5, 6, and 7 are devoted to financial statement analysis. Regardless of your familiarity with financial statements, you will find these chapters useful. I discuss important line items of the financial statements with a focus on determining a company's fiscal strength and if it is moving toward financial distress.

Valuation

The price you pay for a stock determines how much you will profit. As previously stated, this book promotes a value-oriented strategy toward picking stocks. Chapter 8 discusses the two most profitable measures of valuation: price-to-book and price-to-earnings. Chapter 9 discusses discounted future cash flow (DCF), a valuation model commonly used by brokerage analysts. You will learn how it works and its weaknesses.

Creating Your Own Luck

To help you apply the material and create your own customized investment strategy, I have included two additional features in this book. First, at the end of every chapter is a short summary highlighting the key points. These summaries are not meant to replace the material contained in each chapter, but to reinforce what you learned. Secondly, the final chapter provides step-by-step instructions for evaluating your portfolio and analyzing stocks so you can become a smarter investor and create your own luck.

Now let's go make some money.

PART 1

The Investment Community and Your Portfolio:

A Look at the Equity Markets and How to Build a Diversified *Winning* Portfolio

CHAPTER 1

Investment Advice

There is an endless source of investment advice. Analysts, fund managers, websites, newsletters, message boards, and even friends give you an unlimited amount of ideas of how to invest your money.

Some of this advice is good; some of it is not. Some of it is even intended to benefit the information provider, not you, the recipient of the advice.

In theory you could choose to ignore the advice. The downside of doing so, however, is you might miss out on some good advice. Even if 99 of the stocks you hear about are not worth detailed research, one great stock suggestion can make it worthwhile to keep your ears open.

You need to look at any stock or investment option that interests you, then consider the source and why the author recommends it. In this chapter, I discuss some of the major sources of investment advice and explain how you can use their information to your advantage.

Influencing your decision will be information provided by others, including the media, financial professionals, and stock analysts. To make the most effective use of the information provided by these parties, it is useful to understand how these people operate.

BROKERAGE ANALYSTS

The most publicized recommendations come from brokerage analysts. These are people who are specifically hired to make buy or sell recommendations. If they can generate publicity with their recommendations and move the stock price, it is even better because it generates more business for their employer.

These analysts may be referred as "sell-side analysts," because their goal is to get investors—both retail (like you) and institutional—to trade stocks.

When a sell-side analyst issues a report, the report is circulated to the firm's brokers. The brokers, in turn, get on the phone and tell their clients to buy a stock or sell a stock (and buy a different one). In addition, brokers use the reports to tell prospective clients about a hot stock tip. The more people who act on a research report, the more commissions are generated and the more the brokerage firm earns.

Brokerage firms also benefit from their analysts having the ability to influence a stock's price. For instance, when a well-known analyst ups his rating on a stock from "buy" to "strong buy," investors (both clients and non-clients) will rush out and buy, boosting the stock's price. This increases the analyst's reputation as an expert within a particular industry.

Gaining free publicity is good for any business. Not to mention, the more experts a brokerage firm has, the better its ability to attract money management firms, institutional firms, and high net-worth clients. Therefore, while the brokerage analyst's job is to evaluate stocks, the goal behind having a staff of analysts is to generate business.

The downside of this model is the pressure placed on analysts. Many are hesitant to apply a sell rating or its newer equivalent, "underperform." Out of more than 4,200 stocks covered by brokerage analysts in fall 2009, 218 were recommended as "sells" or "strong sells." Conversely, 1,903 were recommended as "strong buy" or "buy" candidates[1]. If they use a sell rating, they will likely face questions about why they used the perceived harsh recommendation. Also, many investors do not want to hear that their stocks should be sold as soon as possible. There are also the corporate executives who push back. It might be a phone call with a complaint or something more drastic, such as refusing to speak to the analyst altogether. Although *Regulation FD*[2] has forced companies

---

[1] *Zacks.com, 2009*

[2] Regulation FD was implemented to force publicly traded companies to give all investors the same access to information impacting a stock's price. Prior to this, many companies shared important information with certain analysts and institutional investors they did not make public. This placed retail investors at an unfair disadvantage and limited market efficiency.

to be more forthcoming, executives can (and likely do) ignore analysts who issue unflattering reports.

As a result, brokerage analyst recommendations are not as powerful as they should or could be. That does not mean the brokerage research has no value; you have to know what to look for.

The first thing is pay attention to the analysts' comments about the company and the industry. Pay particular attention to anything that calls out trends or outside sources. A good analyst will consult outside sources and look for evolving trends. These trends might apply to the company itself (better inventory management) or the entire industry. Identifying these trends and changes in them, can help you make better decisions.

Despite the bias they are exposed to, analysts are smart and inquisitive people. Even if you chose to cast a skeptical eye toward their comments, at least consider the sources they research. Trade publications and surveys are available on the web. If the analysts are reading them, you should too.

Changes in recommendations can be useful. If several brokerage analysts are upgrading or downgrading the stock, there is a reason. It does not matter what the change is (e.g., strong buy to buy or hold to buy), but rather if the recommendations are getting better or worse.

The most effective use of analyst research, though, is the change in consensus earnings estimates. The consensus earnings estimate is the average of all profit forecasts made for a particular company. Though analysts may be wrong in their projection of what a company will earn, they are often right about whether profits will be better or worse than predicted. In addition, it is easier for an analyst to raise his profit forecast than to change a rating.

Magnitude - Consensus Estimate Trend

	Current Quarter (12/2009)	Next Quarter (03/2010)	Current Year (09/2010)	Next Year (09/2011)
Current	2.03	1.71	7.60	9.39
7 Days Ago	1.92	1.59	7.05	8.58
30 Days Ago	1.91	1.56	6.90	8.40
60 Days Ago	1.90	1.53	6.75	7.91
90 Days Ago	1.89	1.53	6.71	7.85

Notice how earning estimates are steadily rising on both a quarterly and an annual basis[3].

---

[3]Consensus earnings estimates for Apple, Inc. (AAPL) courtesy of Zacks.com.

Downgrading a stock will anger clients more so than cutting an earnings estimate will.

In looking at earning estimates, analyze the trend over the last 60 days. Look for a clear trend of rising estimates (good) or falling estimates (bad) and pay attention to the actual size of the changes. A 5-cent change to projected profits of $2 per share (2.5% change) is not as significant as a 5-cent change to projected profits of 50 cents per share (10% change).

Also notice if earning estimates are steadily rising on both a quarterly and an annual basis.

There is a fundamental reason why revisions to earnings estimates help lead to higher stock prices. Stocks are worth what their future profits will be. A company earning $5 per share in the past will not do you any good if the company is now expected to earn $1 per share. The person who sells your stock will value the company based on profits of $1 per share, not $5. When earnings estimates are revised higher, the stock becomes more valuable and its price appreciates.

Changes to earnings estimates can also identify industry trends. This happens when profit projections on several companies within the same industry are revised in the same direction. Such changes tip you off that something positive is occurring. I used upward revisions to identify strong upward moves in copper-related, fertilizer, and semiconductor stocks. In early 2008, downward earnings estimate revisions alerted me to avoid banking stocks.

Keep in mind that changes to earnings estimates will not always call the bottom or the top of a trend; therefore, additional research is needed. Earning estimates can be an effective starting point to conduct further research and are the most effective use of brokerage research.

MONEY MANAGERS

On the other side of brokerage analysts are money managers; people hired to make investment decisions for individuals, pension funds, endowment funds, partnerships, etc. These managers may work for specific clients or, as is the case with mutual funds, for anybody willing to give them money.

Money managers and their analysts are considered to be working on the "buy side," which refers to when professionals make money by investing on behalf of their clients. Rather than trying to sell securities to generate trading commissions, they look for new investment opportunities to buy. Since money managers typically work on a fee basis (clients are charged a percentage of the investments they place with the firm—typically 1-3% of portfolio value), they have little interest in trying to influence the volume or price of a stock.

It is in the best interest of a money management firm not to tell third-parties (and the general public) what investments they are buying. Why? Because they do not want to drive up the price of the stocks they want to buy. An individual buying 100 shares of Toyota (TM) will not have any impact on the price, but a money management firm buying 100,000 shares will. Therefore, it is in the firm's best interest to keep its trading intentions quiet.

So why do portfolio managers speak to the media, publish newsletters or otherwise give out stock tips? Because publicity brings in more assets. If the increase in assets under management exceeds the higher transaction costs caused by the publicity, then the publicity was well worth it. (A transaction cost encompasses fees paid to a broker for trading a stock and the change in price resulting from a transaction.) Remember, money managers make money off of assets under management, so it is in their best interest to bring in more investment dollars.

FINANCIAL ADVISORS

"Financial advisor" is a broad term referring to a person hired to advise a client on managing his portfolio. Advisors can include brokers, financial planners, and other professionals such as CPAs, insurance agents and attorneys.

The term, "stockbroker," has largely faded into the background. Marketing departments for the major brokerage firms have found more success by encouraging individuals to speak with a "financial advisor" than a "broker." Regulatory and industry changes have also played a factor. Most financial advisors are licensed to sell a variety of securities and financial products, including stocks, options, funds, and annuities. Not only does this make it easier for you to manage your finances, it also increases the opportunities of the brokerage firm to sell you an additional product or service.

You may also hear the term, "financial planner." In general, this is mostly a naming convention. The far bigger differences depend on the capacity in which they work. An advisor working for a large brokerage firm will be encouraged to bring as many assets as possible into the firm, whereas an advisor working for himself or a small firm may be content to give you advice on an hourly fee basis without actually making investments for you.

In both cases, training and backgrounds can vary significantly. Some financial advisors have a combination of industry experience, graduate level education, and professional credentials including CFP, CFA, or CPA. Others have little training or industry experience. If they are promoting specific investments, they are required to hold security licenses such as the Series 7 or 63. Keep in mind these licenses are regulatory requirements and do not make the bearer any smarter or talented. Some of the most successful advisors might be good salespeople, while others might not be good at sales but talented at managing money. Many fall somewhere in between and are good at both sales and managing money.

As a rule of thumb, it is better to use an advisor with several years of experience within the financial industry. Such an individual will have seen different market and economic cycles and have an understanding of dealing with bull and bear markets. Keep in mind the experience does not have to come solely from being a financial advisor; the advisor could have also worked in another part of the financial services sector, such as an analyst or a wholesaler.

What you do not want is someone who lacks both experience and an existing set of clients. Such a person may succumb to doing whatever it takes to generate fees and commissions as opposed to looking out for your long-term interests. Do realize, though, that prospecting for new clients is a key part of most financial advisors' jobs. No matter how good they are, there will be turnover in clientele, and as a result, they will need to constantly market to attract new clients.

When choosing a financial advisor consider your needs. What financial products are you looking to invest in: stocks, bonds, annuities, life insurance, etc.? Would you prefer for all of your financial needs (checking, savings, credit cards, loans, investments, etc.) to be handled at a single firm? Are you looking for someone to help you make decisions about investing your money? Do you want to trust that person to make most of the investment decisions for you? Are you reading this book to learn what questions to ask and get an idea of how to monitor what the advisor is doing? Conversely, do you make all of your own investment decisions and want a third-party to give your portfolio a periodic review to make sure your financial decisions are on track? Are there legal or tax issues that need to be handled? Do you need someone who specializes in illiquid investment opportunities such as limited partnerships? Is there a private equity or venture capital opportunity you need help assessing or managing? Or is there something else unique to your situation?

The answers to these questions will determine the advice you need. If you want someone to help make investment decisions, an advisor associated with a brokerage firm might be good. An independent financial advisor might be more willing to meet with you periodically to review your financial situation and make sure you are on track toward your financial goals. A CPA or an estate attorney might be the best financial advisor if you have tax or legal issues.

Depending on your situation, you might find that one person can help with all of your needs or you may need a team of individuals.

Compensation

Financial advisors may charge you commissions, fees, or a combination of the two. Commissions are generated when you buy or sell an investment. Fees are based on the dollar amount invested or time spent consulting with you. Depending on the firm and the account, it is possible for you to pay both commissions (e.g., stock trades) and fees (e.g., mutual fund holdings). Some brokerage firms offer a flat fee with unlimited trades; this avoids a perceived conflict of interest between the broker's recommendation and his compensation.

Many financial advisors, particularly those working for large brokerage firms or banking institutions, are compensated and evaluated according to a grid, which is a list of sales goals the advisor is expected to meet and exceed. For instance, the broker could get extra compensation for getting a certain portion of his book (clients and their accounts) invested in a particular bond fund. Sales managers look at each broker's book to see how well they are selling against the grid. Keep in mind the grid is designed for the employer's best interest, not the client's.

Without asking your advisor about every proposed investment, it is impossible to know what investments are on the grid and which are not. In general, most advisors are good-hearted people who are looking to make a living. They understand it is in their best interest to keep you happy and work for your general benefit. But their first priority is to put food on their tables.

Fees may be charged either as a percentage of assets under management ("AUM") or on an hourly basis. Charging a fee based on AUM ties the advisor's paycheck to the performance of your portfolio. Hourly fees are more often encountered for consultations or when advice is sought for tax or legal advice. You may find yourself paying a combination of commissions and fees.

Though your goal should always be to minimize fees as much as possible, realize the benefit of hiring a quality financial advisor can help you make far more money than you spend on his services. The decision to hire one depends on your financial and legal situation as well as your desire to manage your entire portfolio. There is no right or wrong answer here. You need to do what is best for you.

Financial planners can be compensated based on commissions, fees or a combination of the two. Since financial planners are generally independent, a fee based on a percentage of assets is preferred. Commissions may be acceptable depending on the service provided (e.g., long-term care insurance).

Avoiding Scam Artists

Though the overwhelming majority of financial advisors are honest, there are those who aspire to be the next Bernie Madoff. While Madoff's background set him apart from other Ponzi-scheme operators (Madoff was a former chairman of the NASDAQ), there is usually one red flag that sets them all apart—returns too good to be true.

Madoff succeeded in swindling clients by consistently generating good returns, no matter what market conditions existed. He accomplished this by hiring a staff trained to create account statements that reflected the false performance he claimed to make. Even the most talented money managers lose money.

If the returns look too good to be true, ask to see the annual performance. There should be a mix of good years and not so good years. If the returns look consistently good or consistently stable, be wary. Securities fluctuate in value and so should a financial advisor's performance. If the returns stay consistently good during bull and bear markets, be cautious. Everyone has a bad year sooner or later.

THE MEDIA

There are numerous newspapers, magazines, radio programs, and television shows providing investment advice. There are even cable channels dedicated to investing, such as CNBC, Bloomberg, Fox Business, and BNN

(Canada). The goal of any media outlet is to get people to pay attention, whether that means subscribing, listening or watching. The producers are looking for people who can provide interesting insight into the markets and the economy. The actual information provided by the medium and the outlet varies.

When I appear on TV, I talk to the producer prior to my appearance, going over topics. I will also send talking points with supporting data so the anchor has an idea of what I can talk about and what I cannot. Once I am live on the air, though, I am at the mercy of the anchors who can ask me anything they want. The goal of the anchor is to find a balance between asking the hard questions and keeping the conversation interesting enough for people to watch. My experience has been that television anchors are talented and seek to provide their viewers quality information.

Radio can vary, depending on whether it is live or taped. Wall Street Journal Radio has called me unannounced seeking commentary about what is occurring in the market. I have also done taped radio shows where talking points have been sent over prior to taping. Either way, the journalists I have spoken with have never been afraid to ask tough questions to get the best information for their listeners.

Print media, whether a newspaper or a web column, often results in a longer interview. Often I will be asked a variety of questions and hang up the phone having no idea what the reporter will use. It is not that print journalists are more thorough than their broadcast counterparts, but rather they are not constrained as much by time limitations. What you do not see, though, is the time spent talking with the producer before the live TV or radio interview.

Overall my experience has been that financial journalists are professional and thorough. I have been asked many tough questions and have a lot of respect for what they do.

As far as the people you see on television or quoted in the newspaper, including me, understand they are talking to the masses. The investment advice provided is meant for general consumption and may not be suitable for your specific situation. Still, some good advice is given. If you hear something that interests you, write it down and conduct further research. Never act on advice given through the media but do not ignore it either. The people appearing in the media want you to profit and therefore make every effort to provide quality advice.

WEBSITES, NEWSLETTERS, AND BLOGS

The cost for setting up a website, newsletter or blog is nominal. As a result, there are thousands of options to find stock picks and other investment information on the web. Some of these sources are good and some are bad.

The major financial websites are all generally good. The differences are what they focus on (e.g., news, analysis, data, education, charting). A lot of it depends on personal preference. Though there are advantages to using *Google Finance, Yahoo Finance or Marketwatch.com*, when it comes to the major sites, use whatever site you are comfortable with. I regularly visit about 15 to 20 sites (including *Yahoo Finance and Marketwatch.com*).

The variance in quality increases when you start looking at smaller websites, newsletters, and blogs. Appearance and quality of writing do not provide a good basis for determining what is reputable investment advice. It is inexpensive to hire a good web programmer and a good writer. Therefore, you need to use the stock picks as a starting point for more research. Look at more than one or two stock picks before making a final decision. The author may have gotten lucky with his stock pick or may be experiencing a streak where the market is acting irrationally.

Most importantly, pay attention to the investing philosophy. If you are a value investor looking for long-term investments, spending time on a site oriented toward active trading will not do you much good. You should look for authors whose style of investing is similar to yours, but be willing to read quality commentary from authors with whom you disagree. They might be seeing trends you have missed.

As far as paying for access, that is a personal decision you need to make based on your goals. A lot of great analysis and tools are subscription only; there is also a lot of free information. All of the stock analysis I discuss in Chapters 4 through 9 can be conducted for free. Paying for a screener or an investment newsletter, though, can significantly reduce the number of stocks you have to look at before finding a suitable investment.

SOCIAL NETWORKS AND MESSAGE BOARDS

The web has made it easy for people to share their viewpoints about stocks: message boards, online community forums, and social networking sites, such as Facebook and Twitter, make it easier for investors to get together.

The inherent problem is you do not know who is posting the information or how reputable the information is. Even if somebody claims to be an employee or possess some other type of insight, there is no guarantee. In addition, a well-written post can be recommended, even if its analysis is completely wrong.

Some sites are trying to resolve this problem by ranking members on the quality of their picks. The upshot is you have a gauge to determine who is picking good stocks. The downside is the other person may be following a strategy that is unsuitable for you or worse, happens to be lucky with his picks.

Therefore, I would view these forums as a method to interact with other investors. Try out new ideas, talk up your current stock picks and see what others are doing. Do not invest in any stock because it was mentioned on a message board. Do your research first to make sure the Risk-Reward Ratio is in your favor.

INVESTMENT SEMINARS

Investment seminars have been around for decades. Financial planners will use them to find new clients. They will talk about a topic of interest (e.g., retirement planning), hoping a few members of the audience will invest with them. Other companies use seminars to sell workshops and tools. For instance, INVESTools puts on free seminars to promote its products. These seminars are marketing pitches to get attendees to register for a workshop.

If the seminar is free, it is probably a marketing pitch. This does not mean good information will not be provided or you should not go, but set your expectations accordingly. Many financial advisors will provide useful information about portfolio management and retirement planning. If you do not mind a follow-up call a few days later, attend the event.

As far as paying for a full seminar, ask yourself if what is being promoted matches your style of investing. Presenters make it look easy to make money in the market—that is what they are hired to do. The reality is if you follow the system, you will have losing trades. Even if the system works overall, you will not be likely to follow it if you are required to trade more often or frequently than you like. Most two- or three-day seminars involve active trading and often options trading. Trading seminars attract more people than investing seminars, even though most people would be better off trading less frequently and spending more time applying the Risk-Reward Ratio. Use your judgment.

Do not be afraid to pay for a seminar, but do so because you are truly interested, not because you think doing so will make you rich.

KEY CHAPTER POINTS

1. Brokerage analyst recommendations are not as powerful as they should or could be. Rather than pay attention to whether a stock is rated a "buy" or a "hold," check to see if the average recommendation is improving or worsening.

2. The most effective use of brokerage analyst research is the change in the consensus earnings estimate. A clear trend of rising earnings estimates over the last 60 days is preferable.

3. Financial advisors can be helpful, but consider your needs before choosing one.

4. The investment advice the media provides may not be suitable to your specific situation. If you hear something that sounds interesting, write it down and conduct more research before making a decision to invest.

5. Much information can be found on the web, but the quality can vary significantly. Furthermore, particularly on social websites and message boards, you often do not know who is posting or their reputability. Even if a post appears to be well written, it can contain erroneous information.

CHAPTER 2

Portfolio Theory and Management

How you establish and manage your portfolio will have a significant impact on how much your wealth increases over time. Too often, people think of portfolio management as picking the right stocks or correctly timing the market. Worse, many investors do not give much thought to constructing their portfolios.

This is a shame because decisions you make in managing your portfolio determine how much risk you are exposing yourself to and how much money you are losing in transaction costs.

Though you may have multiple portfolios, such as a brokerage account, a 401K plan, employee stock options or other assets, understand they all contribute to your overall wealth. Why you might think of decisions made in your 401K plan as different from those in your trading account, they are one and the same. At the end of the day, your net wealth is determined by the dollar value of all your investments, be it stocks or art. Furthermore, if you start thinking about your accounts as one large portfolio, you can make decisions that may even lower your tax bill—something everyone likes.

There are two primary aspects to portfolio management to focus on—asset allocation and transaction costs. Asset allocation is more than "diversification," it is about the securities in your portfolio, how they work together, and what your personal financial needs are. Transaction costs are what you pay in fees to invest; these include brokerage commissions, mutual fund fees, and trading costs.

ASSET ALLOCATION

Asset allocation is at the heart of the Risk-Reward Ratio. At any stage in life, you want to maximize returns while controlling the risk of losing money. At the basic level you need to determine what percentage of your investment dollars should be allocated to stocks, bonds, commodities, real estate, alternative assets (e.g., antiques, vintage watches), and cash.

The decision on allocating your investment dollars depends on your age, income, and financial needs. A single person in his or her twenties and in good health, should place an emphasis on stocks while mixing in a small percentage of Treasury bonds, junk bonds, and commodities. A person near retirement with health issues should keep the majority of his or her assets in money market accounts and high-grade bonds, which offer access to cash when needed. The rule of thumb is the longer the period of time before you need access to the money, the greater the risk you can take with investments. Cash needed within the next one to three years should never be invested in stocks. Conversely, if your time horizon is 20 years or more, stocks should be used so your portfolio will increase at a rate above that of inflation.

Also consider your personal financial situation. A recently retired individual with a large amount of wealth can maintain a greater allocation to stocks than a similar individual who was never able to save as much. The wealthier individual is better able to withstand a downturn in the financial markets than someone who either needs to protect a nest egg or face the prospect of coming out of retirement.

A good financial planner can help determine how to allocate your portfolio, though there are also various tools and guides on the web.

DIVERSIFICATION AND THE EFFICIENT MARKET FRONTIER

Though a large part of asset allocation is determining what asset classes are suitable for your age and financial situation, another component needs to be factored—how those asset classes and the underlying individual securities work together. This is where Modern Portfolio Theory comes into play.

In 1952, Noble Laureate Harry Markowitz theorized that investing in several risky assets could reduce overall portfolio risk. In other words, by combining several different investments together, the overall risk of the portfolio is lower than of the underlying securities themselves.

That might sound confusing, so we will look at a simplistic portfolio comprised of two fictional stocks. The first stock is Bankruptcy Liquidators. This company enjoys substantial profits during economic downturns. When the economy is doing well, bankruptcy filings decline and so do the company's profits. The second stock is Risky Creditors. This company lends money to almost anybody. During times of economic expansion, people take out more loans and pay their bills. When the economy takes a downturn, bills go unpaid, hurting profits.

If a 10-year chart of both stocks were created, it might look like this:

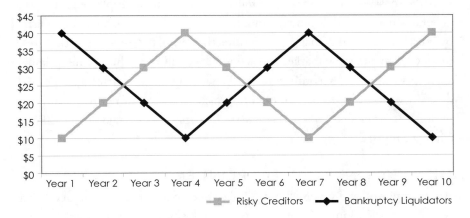

As you can see, both stocks are volatile. Buying either stock at the wrong time could result in a loss of money. However, the two stocks move in completely opposite directions. When shares of Bankruptcy Liquidators take a dive, shares of Risky Creditors do quite well, and vice versa.

Putting both stocks in a portfolio, though, results in a stable return. Why? Because when one stock falls, the other rises. Therefore, as long as both stocks move in equal, but opposite directions, an investor will earn a return reflecting the average of the increase in value of one and the decline in price for the other. In reality, it is impossible to find two stocks moving in directly opposite

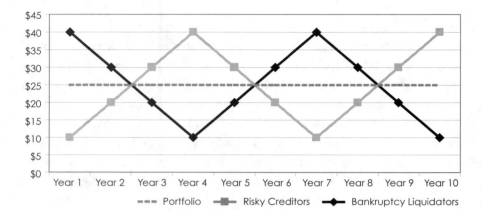

directions over a long period of time. Furthermore, only keeping two stocks in a portfolio is extremely risky. If one company goes under, then half of the portfolio's value will be wiped out.

It is possible to create a portfolio comprised of multiple securities that generates both a higher return and a lower level of risk. This is accomplished by purchasing stocks that are not directly correlated—meaning they react differently to changing market and economic conditions. This is what is known as diversification. According to Markowitz, when a portfolio is properly diversified, an investor has achieved the maximum level of return for any level of risk. In academic books, this is described as investing along the Efficient Market Frontier.

THE EFFICIENT MARKET FRONTIER

An example of a diversified portfolio is one that contains Treasury bonds, corporate bonds, industrial stocks, technology stocks, financial stocks, energy stocks, international stocks, real estate, and gold. Except for periods of extreme financial duress, not all of these assets will change in price at the same time or at the same degree. As a result, some of the assets should, theoretically, rise in price at any time. The biggest benefit to diversification is it will reduce the chances of an economic downturn destroying your net worth.

The other benefit to diversification is boosting your returns. By investing along the Efficient Market Frontier, Markowitz theorized an investor will achieve the maximum level of return for the level of risk accepted. By grouping together uncorrelated assets, the risk of the portfolio will be reduced. Another reason is some part of the portfolio will be in favor at any time. It might be that money is flowing to bonds and out of commodities or technology stocks are looked upon favorably. By staying diversified, you can take advantage of these trends and offset lagging performance by another stock or class of assets in your portfolio.

When Markowitz unveiled his theory in 1952, the financial community was shocked. Stocks at that time were considered to be risky and not suitable for many individual investors. Financial planners advised investing primarily in bonds unless an individual had a lot of wealth. With the advent of discount brokerage firms, mutual funds and exchange-traded funds, this has all changed. Investors now have access to a variety of asset classes, which can improve your risk-adjusted returns.

OTHER CONSIDERATIONS

There are two other aspects regarding asset allocation not receiving the focus they should: real estate and your job.

Real Estate

If you own a house or a condominium, you have an allocation to residential real estate. Chances are it is your single-largest investment. Also, if you have a mortgage, your investment is leveraged, meaning it is partially owned by the lenders. As many homeowners found out in 2008 and 2009, a house can drop significantly in value.

Because you need a place to live, there is a pragmatic reason to invest in real estate, but you do not have to invest in homebuilders or companies dependent on the strength of the housing sector. Doing so increases your allocation to real estate and the potential risk of losing more money in a downturn.

I'm not saying you should avoid homebuilders, building supply companies, home improvement retailers or banks because you own a house. But you should take it into consideration, especially if you live in a key market for that company. Even though physical real estate and stocks are two different securities, the macroeconomic factors affecting the value of your house could also impact the stock prices of companies within the housing sector. Alternatively, you could consider Real Estate Investment Trusts (REITs) that focus on commercial real estate or companies whose key geographic markets are different than the metropolitan area you live in.

Your Employer

Your company may offer you stock options, stock, or a discounted stock purchase plan as part of a compensation package. These plans may contribute to your overall compensation. Participating in such plans may be encouraged by the corporate climate or, if you are high enough in the company, by the shareholders.

When considering an investment stake in your company, balance what is good for your job with what is good for your overall portfolio. Accepting stock options or participating in an employee stock option plan (ESOP) may increase your compensation. Some employers offer stocks instead of a higher direct salary. On the other hand, every dollar you invest in your employer increases your overall financial risk. If the company hits a rough spot, both your compensation and the value of your investment could decrease. In a worse-case scenario, such as Enron, you could lose both your job and your investment in the company.

In terms of options and stock grants, the prudent move is to sell them as quickly as possible. If you think the company is doing great and the stock price will go higher, set a minimum price where you will exercise your options and sell your stock (e.g., 10% below the current price). Also consider the liquidity of your equity stake in the company. There may be certain rules impacting when you can exercise the options or sell the shares. If you have the option of receiving cash or employee stock in a retirement plan, opt for the cash unless there is an overriding reason to take the stock (e.g., not accepting the stock will be heavily frowned upon by your manager or the CEO).

The same advice goes for investing in companies operating in the same sector as your employer. Although you may know the industry inside and out, a shift in business conditions affecting your employer can also impact your employer's competitors, customers, and suppliers. There is no reason to risk losing a paycheck while seeing the value of your portfolio decline.

If your company is not publicly traded, you have another situation to deal with—valuation. There is no listed share price on an exchange so the value of your investment is determined by an outside consultant, such as a business valuation specialist or, if the company is a start-up, a venture capitalist. In such cases, look to diversify your other investments into industries and sectors outside the one you work in.

Do not turn down the opportunity to invest in your company, especially if it is offered as part of your compensation package, but do understand the risks.

Make sure your wealth and your salary are not dependent on the same industry, whenever possible.

TRANSACTION COSTS

Though a lot of emphasis is placed on diversification, transaction costs do not receive the scrutiny they should. Every dollar you save on transaction costs is an extra dollar in your pocket. Over time, these savings can have a significant impact on your wealth.

A transaction cost is any expense incurred in the transfer of assets. A transaction cost can be direct, such as a brokerage commission for buying or selling a stock, or it can be indirect, such as a mutual fund management fee. All transaction costs adversely affect the real return a portfolio generates.

Brokerage Commissions

Transaction costs are thought of in terms of brokerage commissions: the cost of executing a trade. A discount broker may charge $10 or less to execute a stock trade. To buy and sell a specific stock, an investor would incur a transaction cost of $20. However, the actual transaction costs may be greater.

Consider a stock that was purchased at $50 and then sold at $55. The investor's return on such a purchase would be 10%, if no transaction costs were incurred. With transaction costs, his return is less. To explain why, let's use a trade involving 100 shares.

The purchase price is $5,000 (100 shares at $50 per share). The sell price is $5,500 (100 shares at $55 per share). The gross gain on the purchase is $500 ($5,500 - $5,000 = $500). Assuming a commission of $10 per trade, the gain is reduced to $480 ($500 less $10 for buying the stock and an additional $10 for selling the stock). As a result, the profit you see in your brokerage account is not $500, but $480. Although the stock increased in value by 10% ($50 to $55), the actual gain you realized is just 9.6% ($480 profit divided by the original investment of $5,000). This means your performance was 40 basis points (0.4%) less than the amount the stock actually appreciated.

This might not seem like much, especially when talking about a 0.4% difference, but over the long-term, the difference can be substantial. Say you have $50,000 to invest. Losing 0.4% in transaction costs can result in more than $4,000 of potential profits you will never realize over a period of 20 years.

Capital Gains Taxes

Depending on one's tax bracket, a large percentage of profits can be forfeited to taxes. For example, at a 25% tax rate, you would only realize 7.5% of every 10% move in a stock. Your profit would also be reduced by brokerage costs for making the trade.

Individual investors can control transaction costs by selecting stocks to hold for the long-term. Limiting the amount of trades reduces both the brokerage commissions and tax rate. Long-term capital gains are taxed at a lower rate than short-term gains, an instant profit.

Taxes can also be managed by avoiding the wash sale rule. The wash sale rule kicks in when you sell a stock or security at a loss. If you buy a substantially identical security within the next 30 days, you cannot deduct the loss. For example, say a stock is sold at a loss on March 1. On March 27, the company releases good news and you decide to repurchase the stock. Under IRS rules, you cannot deduct the previous (March 1) loss from your taxes. As result, the wash sale can actually increase the amount of taxes you pay[1].

Trading Costs

Trading costs refers to the ability to buy or sell at the quoted price. This expense is dependent on the volume of the transaction relative to the average number of shares bought and sold on a given day. A disproportionately large order will cause the price to change, thereby increasing the cost of the transaction. In simplistic terms, if your attempt to buy or sell a stock changes the share price, you are paying a trading cost.

For the average individual, trading costs will be minimal if fairly liquid[2] stocks are targeted. Buying or selling 100 or even 1,000 shares of General Electric (GE) will not move its price, because nearly 100 million shares are traded on an average day. Buying or selling 1,000 shares in a stock with an average volume of 10,000 shares a day, though, could cause the price to move because there are not as many buyers and sellers. The greater the average daily volume, the more likely you will be able to buy or sell at the quoted price.

---

[1] Read IRS Publication 550 for a full explanation of the wash sale rule, including which securities are covered by it and which are not.
[2] Liquidity refers to the ease of buying or selling an asset. The smaller the number of buyers and sellers for a given asset, the less liquid it is. Shares of a Dow Jones Industrial Average stock are very liquid because of the large number of buyers and sellers and an easily identifiable price. An antique vase is illiquid because of the relatively small amount of buyers and sellers and the lack of an identifiable price.

Institutional investors spend a lot of time analyzing trading costs. They realize they cannot conduct a transaction involving hundreds of thousands of shares at once. Therefore, they space out their orders over a period of days or even weeks—depending on the stock's average volume and size of the order. They realize they will gain more from not moving the price than trying to complete the order at once.

An imbalance between buyers and sellers can also drive up trading costs, which happens when there is breaking news about the stock. If there is a significant imbalance between the number of buyers and sellers, the exchange can halt trading. Trading is then suspended until a price attracting enough buyers and sellers can be determined. Often the stock re-opens for trading at a price notably different from what it sold for in the last trade before the halt.

You can often see the impact of trading imbalances on charts. Look for gaps, as is shown in this chart of American International Group (AIG).

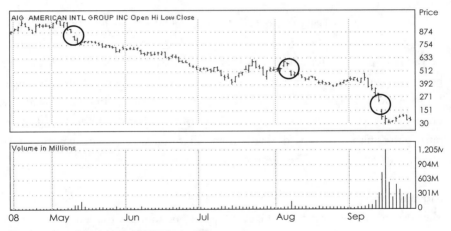

Chart courtesy of QuoteMedia. ©2010 Quotemedia.

As long as you focus on stocks and exchange-traded funds with a sizable amount of average daily volume, your trading costs will not be a concern. As a rule of thumb always look for daily average volume in excess of 100,000 shares per day. An alternative method is to calculate the average daily volume in terms of total dollars; multiply the average number shares traded by the current share price. Such a method works well when evaluating a stock with a low price (e.g., Cosi, Inc. (COSI)) or a very high price (e.g,. Berkshire-Hathaway (BRK.A)). When I was at Zacks, we followed a general guideline for our picks: average daily volume must equate to at least $1 million per day.

If a stock has low volume, you may face a notable difference between the bid (what buyers will pay) and the ask price (what sellers want). Using a limit order and telling the broker the entire order does not need to be filled at once will help lower the trading cost. Understand, though, you may not be able to buy all of the shares you want or, worse, be able to sell all of your position at a price you prefer.

Exchange-Traded Fund Fees

Exchange-Traded Funds (ETFs) allow you to buy into a portfolio of stocks. The portfolio is based on an index, such as the S&P 500. ETFs track an index so the management fees[3] are low, often below 0.5%. In addition, the transaction costs related to the fund are low due to low turnover (changes are only made when an index is rebalanced). Compared to the alternative of buying a basket of stocks, ETFs can be cost effective, especially if you want to track the entire market or specific sectors.

There are a few caveats to ETFs. The actual index used by an ETF is selected by the fund manager. As a result, even similar ETFs can have different holdings or give greater emphasis to certain stocks. If the ETF uses futures or holds foreign stocks, the management fee can also be higher. Finally, leveraged ETFs—those designed to change in price twice or three times as fast as the underlying index—can also have tracking error. This means the actual long-term performance may be different than what you would have expected. As result, your returns could be significantly impacted.

Mutual Fund Fees

The costs for mutual funds can be even higher. In addition to management fees, 12b-1 (marketing) fees can be levied. Some funds may also charge a load, which is a a fee for buying or selling shares. Although no-load funds have been popularized in the press, a front-load fund (pay a charge for buying shares) or an end-load fund (pay a charge for selling shares) may be cheaper. It depends on the fund.

Then there is the tax issue. Every mutual fund comes with embedded gains. An embedded gain is an unrealized profit on assets held by the fund. For instance, say a mutual fund buys shares of stock XYZ at $20. Six months later, the shares rise to $25. During the sixth month, a new investor buy shares in the fund. In

---

[3] Management fees cover the cost of operating the fund, including salaries, overhead, research, customer service, and other expenses.

month seven, the mutual fund manager decides to sell the stock at $25. The new investor is suddenly faced with having to pay taxes on the $5 gain in the stock.

Why? Mutual funds are required to pass on all capital gains and losses to their shareholders. Since a gain or loss is not realized until the asset is sold, the investor responsible for paying the tax is the one who held shares at the time of the transaction. Compounding matters, shareholders have no idea what the amount of embedded gains a mutual fund has at any time and have no control over when a fund manager sells a stock. It is possible to see the value of your mutual fund shares decline and still have to pay capital gains taxes on the mutual fund's transactions[4].

The extent to which these costs can add up may be surprising. Data from the research firm Lipper suggests investors have seen their actual stock-oriented mutual fund returns reduced by 250 basis points or more because of expenses and taxes[5]. This means instead of the theoretical 10% return reported by a fund, you may only realize a return of 7.5%. That is a big difference.

Other Costs

Your brokerage firm may charge custodial or account maintenance fees. These are charges for keeping an account open and cover the expenses of overhead, bookkeeping and liability. If these fees allow you to pay lower commissions, speak with a good financial advisor or access quality research; they may be worth the cost. But ask yourself if you are getting the perceived value in exchange for those fees.

Advisory fees are charges for consulting with a financial professional and receiving his input. Many advisors charge an annual fee based on the size of the portfolio (often in a range of 1% to 3%). Such an arrangement can be beneficial to the investor because the advisor's income is dependent on the performance of the portfolio—the more money you make, the more the advisor makes. But the quality of the advice and the performance should justify the fee.

Fees can also be levied for purchasing shares on a foreign exchange,

---

[4] A mutual fund's price is determined at the close of each trading day. If a mutual fund previously performed well and then declined in value, a manager may choose to sell assets and take profits while he can. An investor who was unlucky enough to buy the mutual fund at its high would see the value of his investment decline. In addition, because the mutual fund manager is selling assets, the investor would have to pay the capital gains taxes on those embedded gains. This was a reality that many investors faced following the burst of the tech bubble.

[5] Taxes In The Mutual Fund Industry—2009, Lipper, April 2009, *www.lipperweb.com/Handlers/GetReport. ashx?reportId=1913*

transferring assets from one brokerage firm to another, check-writing privileges or receiving physical certificates.

Periodically review all the fees and determine if they are justified. Although every dollar in fees paid is a dollar you will not see again, the value you receive for spending extra money may offset the cost. This is the case when expenditures result in a better risk-adjusted return than you would have achieved by going for the lowest cost investment options. Also consider external factors, such as whether you want your brokerage office to have a physical location or have other financial service needs (e.g., money market accounts, estate planning issues), making it wiser to bundle your accounts with a specific firm.

ACTIVE VS. PASSIVE

When considering how to diversify your portfolio and manage your transaction costs, decide whether you want to actively or passively manage your portfolio. Following an active strategy means directly selecting the individual securities or hiring someone, such as a mutual fund manager, to do so. A passive strategy means you are content to follow an index, such as the S&P 500. There are advantages and disadvantages to both.

Active

Active strategies involve picking every security for your portfolio, which allows you to determine the level of risk. By selecting conservative assets, you could create a portfolio with lower risk than one that tracks the S&P 500. Similarly, you could elect to take on additional risk, hoping to achieve higher returns. Active investing also allows you to overweight specific sectors and styles of assets.

For instance, if you think mid-cap oil stocks are going to perform well over the next six months, by using an active strategy, you can allocate a greater portion of your portfolio to such stocks.

Most importantly, active investing provides the opportunity to generate a return in excess of the market return. This outperformance is known as "alpha." Alpha is the proportion of a portfolio's return attributable to your, or a money manager's, stock-picking abilities; i.e., the return generated in excess of what the portfolio should have generated based on its risk profile.

The problem with an active strategy is it is difficult to consistently generate alpha. Most money managers do not outperform the S&P 500 over long periods. If the wrong stocks are selected, a portfolio's returns can lag the return that would have been achieved by following a passive strategy. Too much risk may be taken on for the level of returns achieved.

Passive

A passive strategy involves tracking market indexes. For instance, you could buy the S&P 500 SPDR (SPY), which generates a return similar to that of the S&P 500.

There are advantages to a passive strategy. The passive approach eliminates the risk of picking the wrong stocks. The stocks are automatically selected based on the composition of the index; therefore no additional human input is required. Diversification is provided by the sheer number of stocks—most major market indexes are comprised of hundreds of shares.[6] The large number of stocks within the portfolio reduces the chances that any one stock will wreck the return.

Transaction costs are limited and a passive strategy ensures you will always be invested in the market. This means you will always be poised to take advantage of any large gains and your losses will be limited to those of the market.[7]

The problem with a passive investment strategy is it limits you to whatever performance the market generates. If the S&P 500 rises 10%, you earn 10%. If the S&P 500 falls 10%, then you lose 10%. The actual returns may not always match, though, because of tracking error. Tracking error is the difference between the return of an index and a portfolio designed to mimic that index. Any difference between the proportionate holdings of each member stock, the timing each stock is added to the index and the index fund, cash held in the index fund, and transaction costs (which are not factored into index returns) will result in tracking error. It is impossible to avoid tracking error, though some fund companies have done a great job of limiting it.

---

[6] The Dow Jones Industrial Average is the notable exception. This index only has 30 stocks, but these are generally stable, large-cap companies.

[7] There is always a risk of financial problems at the management company operating the passive investment strategy. In a severe market crash, the management company may not be able to raise funds quickly enough to pay all investors who want to get out of the market. Safeguards are built into the markets to prevent this from occurring and a large firm should have systems in place to handle such a scenario, but the risk cannot be eliminated. Unfortunately, the only way to avoid this risk is to put your money inside a mattress. Management companies from time to time do run into financial problems, so it is important to inquire about the financial stability of any asset management company (e.g., a mutual fund, a hedge fund, a financial advisor), before handing over your money.

Active or Passive – Which Do You Choose?

Part of the decision in determining whether to use an active or passive strategy is how efficient you think the markets are. If you think the markets are always right, then follow a passive strategy. If you think you can do a better job of selecting stocks than the pros, follow an active strategy. This does not have to be an either-or decision. You should consider using a combination of the two.

The argument for passive investing is based on Eugene Fama's Efficient Market Hypothesis (EMH). Fama, a professor at the University of Chicago, theorized stock prices reflect all known information. Furthermore, prices rapidly react to factor in any new information and the timing of new information is random. Finally, the theory assumes investors act rationally to maximize profits.

The biggest argument against EMH is the list of people who have created great wealth over time. For instance, Warren Buffett would not be a household name if EMH held true. Another argument is investors and financial professionals do not always act rationally. We witnessed this with the bursting of the housing bubble and resulting credit crunch. The demographic data existed to show many of the loans had a high probability of default, but many financial professionals let greed interfere with what should have been rational decision making.

By combining active and passive management strategies, you can take advantage of both their strengths. For example, it is unlikely your research will uncover anything about Johnson & Johnson (JNJ) that thousands of others do not know. But you may determine that sentiment toward health care stocks is pessimistic and valuations appear cheap.

Another reason to combine both strategies: you benefit from selecting the right stocks while protecting yourself from mistakes. If you conduct the analysis I discuss in the following chapters, you will increase your odds of picking a stock that will more likely appreciate than decline in value. Sooner or later you will pick the wrong stock, but by combining active and passive strategies, you may beat the market while still having a portion of your portfolio earning a rate of return similar to the market. You are giving your portfolio an insurance policy while still maintaining the flexibility to go after bigger returns. Worst-case scenario: You will know part of your portfolio is tracking the markets. Best-case scenario: you will achieve greater wealth while controlling your risk.

KEY CHAPTER POINTS

1. All your investments—including your brokerage account, a 401K plan, employee and stock options—contribute to your overall wealth and should be managed as a single portfolio.

2. The decision on allocating your investment dollars depends on your age, income, and financial needs.

3. You can lower the overall risk of your portfolio by combing several different investments.

4. Every dollar you save on transaction costs increases your portfolio return. Over time, these savings can have a significant impact on your wealth. But the value you receive for spending extra money on transaction costs may offset the cost.

5. Consider using a combination of active and passive strategies. Doing so allows you to benefit from the potential upside of selecting the right stocks while protecting yourself from your own mistakes.

CHAPTER 3

Psychology, Social Investing, and Sentiment

How you invest is nearly as important as what you invest in. If you make the wrong decision, it is easy to correct your mistake; sell the stock. Hold onto a stock longer than you should and you could incur a big loss. Take an unnecessary risk and you may need more time to regain the lost wealth. Do something that goes against your values and you will struggle with your conscience.

The best investors and traders are unemotional. Every investment is a business deal—a means to make money. These successful people do make mistakes, a lot of them, but they also know how to cut their losses. More importantly, they learn from their mistakes.

If you can learn to control your emotions, make rational decisions, and be willing to part with an investment, you will increase your overall returns. Even if you think of yourself as a "buy-and-hold investor," you should be willing to sell a stock at a moment's notice. Business and investing conditions change, so should your portfolio.

This chapter will focus on how to make rational investment decisions. I will show you how to keep your emotions at bay, align your moral beliefs with your investing style, and how to use charts, which are important if you rely on fundamental analysis to make buy-and-sell decisions.

THE PSYCHOLOGY OF INVESTING

A great deal of research has been conducted into behavioral science and investing. Researchers want to know how emotions and personality affect investment decisions. Considering the trillions of dollars invested worldwide, these studies make sense. Even a small change in the decision-making process could result in a notable increase in portfolio performance.

Think about your emotions when you make a new investment. If you are like most investors, you may be nervous about a new stock. You hope you made the right decision and the stock will go up. You might even think you figured how to beat the market, or at least take advantage of its current conditions.

What about when it is time to sell? If you have a profit, you may be worried about selling too early. Perhaps the stock can trade even higher. Or maybe you are mad at yourself for not selling at the peak. On the other hand, if you have a loss, you may be upset and vow not to make the same mistake again. You could even be angry at the markets, the company's executives, professional traders, your broker or anybody else who caused you to lose money; that is okay.

Investing is an emotional experience. It feels great when your stocks are rising and terrible when your stocks are falling. There is no amount of research and nothing I can say to remove those feelings. What behavioral science hopes to create, though, are methods to keep your emotions from interfering with your buy-and-sell decisions.

Fortunately, you do not have to read through pages of academic material to keep your emotions in check. A few simple rules will improve your decision-making process.

The #1 Rule of Investing:
Only do what allows you to sleep at night.

Investing is a means to an end. It is a process meant to increase your wealth. Being a successful investor will not get you more friends, help you enjoy your family more or make you happier. It will not improve your health. But it can give you greater access to all of these things. But that is all.

Sleep, on the other hand, has a range of physical, mental, and emotional benefits. Sleep can help you become a better investor. But investing will not make you a better sleeper. So do not hold onto any investment that keeps you awake at night—whether you are stressed about losing money or giddy about the money you are making. It does not matter how profitable an investment is, if you do not feel comfortable owning the stock, do not buy it.

Chances are your intuition will tell you in what you should invest. It could be something you read in this book. It could be a lesson from another investment you made. Or it could be your judgment signaling something does not seem right. Even if it is only what risk you are or are not willing to take, do what is best for you.

With thousands of stocks and investment opportunities, not every one is going to be for you. If a stock is keeping you awake at night, sell it and find something else to invest in. You will be happier; that is what is important.

Keep an Investing Journal

I am a big believer in keeping a journal of all investment decisions. I used a spiral notebook to manage the model portfolios for *Zacks.com*. Even though I do most of my research online, I keep a journal. A simple spiral notebook is the most important investment tool I have.

Take a look at your current portfolio. Can you tell me why you bought each stock? This is no small question because the other big rule of investing is to sell when the reason you bought the stock no longer applies. But if you do not write that down, how will you remember what it was?

You could trust your memory, but consider how many other things you need to remember: milk at the grocery store; your spouse's birthday; a doctor's appointment; setting up a meeting. You have a lot to think about, even without considering your portfolio. So why try to cram more in your brain and hope you can remember that critical piece of information?

Let's take this a step further. The stock you held for a year is starting to drop in price. Do you sell or hold onto it? If you kept an investing journal, you would have a set of notes explaining why you bought it. Maybe the stock was undervalued or business was expanding. Maybe the industry was in a turnaround. If you have your rationale recorded, you will be able to see if it applies. Often the reasons you bought the stock will not apply. If so, then you need to evaluate if you would buy the stock today if you did not own it. Many times, you would not—a sign it is time to sell.

A more effective way to use the journal is to list factors causing you to sell the stock before you buy it. This could be a price target, potential changes in business conditions, a merger or a shift in market conditions. It is better to outline these reasons before buying the stock because you will not be emotionally attached to the investment. When you own the stock, you will be able to look at your list and consult pre-established guidelines for determining when to sell.

Use Price Limits

No matter how much research you do or how good your analysis is, a stock will act in an unexpected manner. It could drop dramatically, suffer a slow decline in price or surge. How you deal with the price action will affect your wealth.

STRATEGIES TO HELP YOU

The 10-20 Rule

The 10-20 rule kicks in when a stock unexpectedly declines in price. The numbers represent percentages: a 10% loss and a 20% loss.[1]

If a stock declines 10% from my purchase price, I reevaluate the investment decision. I rerun my analysis as if I were buying the stock for the first time and determine if I missed something. It may be a damaging news story, a competitor who said industry conditions were worsening or I misread the financial statements. Something may have changed from when I bought the stock and I did not notice the change until the re-evaluation.

Often the re-evaluation will support my decision to buy the stock. The 10% drop, though unpleasant, was a sign I bought too early. Since investing is not precise, mistiming a buying opportunity will happen. Even the most successful traders find themselves buying too early or too late. If the analysis is correct, the 10% drop will not matter because the stock will bounce back and you will be on your way to greater wealth.

Your goal is not to find the lowest price, but to find a price low enough to warrant holding onto the stock. If your analysis is correct, you will rarely see a drop of 10%; instead you will realize significant profits.

Sometimes the stock will continue dropping. This can occur even when your analysis is right and you know you made the right decision. This is when the other half of the 10-20 rule kicks in. Sell any stock that falls by 20%, no matter how right you are about the stock; if it falls by 20%, sell it. Do not ask any questions. Do not do any further research. Sell the stock.

---

[1] There is nothing magical about these numbers, though they are slightly greater than the average market correction and bear market declines, respectively. You can make the stops tighter. The key point is to have a target that causes you to redo your analysis and a second target that causes you so sell the stock regardless of how correct your analysis is.

There are times when the market moves against you. (The market can stay irrational longer than you can remain solvent.) There will also be periods when you are unlucky. If you try to fight the bad luck, you will end up losing more money. It is better to cut your losses. You can always buy the stock back at a later date once it has stopped its decline.

Sell Half on a Double

This rule kicks in when your stock doubles in price. If the stock rises 100% and you sell half of your position, you will get back all the money you originally invested. As a result, the only risk you have is losing your profits, not your initial investment.

Say you buy 100 shares of a stock trading at $50, a $5,000 investment. Your timing is perfect and a year later the stock is trading $100 per share. If you sell 50 shares, you will get the original $5,000 investment back. As a result, the most you could lose is the $5,000 in profits you still have in the stock. (50 shares at $100 per share.) Regardless of what happens in the future, you took your original $5,000 investment out of the stock.[2]

Trailing Stops

If a stock makes a sharp run over a shorter period, I consider selling or reducing the number of shares I hold; for example, when a stock jumps by 30% in a week or 50% in four months. (I have seen both happen.) If the valuation is still attractive and the business still good, I may use a trailing stop instead, which means selling the stock if it drops by 10% or more. I let the stock continue to rise, but I keep raising the price at which I will sell. The goal is to maximize the profit without being too greedy.

Say a stock jumps from $25 to $40 in a few months. I will set a trailing stop at $36 per share, which is 10% below the $40 price. As long as the stock stays above $36, I will hold onto it. If the stock drops to $36, I will sell it. If the stock rises to $44, I will increase my trailing stop to $39.60, or 10% below $44. Every time the stock sets a new high, I will increase the trailing stop. This allows me to enjoy the upward move without having to worry about selling the stock too late.

---

[2]Note that when you factor in commissions and taxes, you may receive less than the full $5,000 in proceeds. Nonetheless, as long as you sell the remainder of your position before the stock loses most (e.g., 70%) or more of its value, you will receive all of your original investment.

There is no magic to any of these numbers and you can adjust them. The purpose is to set limits to keep your emotions out of buy-and-sell decisions.

Earnings Estimates

Monitoring changes in earnings estimates will improve the timing of your buy-and-sell decisions; they can even save you from losing most of your money.

In February 2008, I warned investors about problems with American International Group (AIG)[3]. The firm revealed in a SEC filing that its internal model underestimated losses for two subsidiaries. AIG said the new calculations suggested a potential loss of $5 billion, instead of an actual loss of $1.6 billion. My warning did not come from hours of research or in-depth knowledge about AIG, but from a downward revision to full-year profit projections. I saw the cut to the Zacks Consensus Estimate and read news articles and SEC filings to determine what was behind the downward revision. In 10 minutes, I knew there was something wrong with AIG. Even if someone did not react to the initial cuts, the subsequent downward revisions would have been a big, flashing sign to sell the stock.

Earnings Estimate and Price Changes for AIG[4]

Date	2008 EPS Estimate	Stock Price
2/19/2008	$6.62	$47.03
3/18/2008	$5.15	$43.67
4/16/2008	$4.29	$45.47
5/15/2008	$4.01	$39.57
6/17/2008	$3.04	$32.28
7/15/2008	$2.58	$20.64
8/19/2008	$0.20	$20.32
9/16/2008	-$0.81	$3.75

You should not be concerned with the actual consensus estimate but rather the trend. Rising earnings estimates signal that business is better than previously thought. Falling earnings estimates signal that business is worse than previously thought. Brokerage analysts might be lousy at making price targets, but they do an effective job of identifying whether their forecasts are too optimistic or too pessimistic. (Keep in mind, however, that any forecast is subject to human error.)

When looking at earnings estimate revision trends, consider the size of the change, the proportion of covering analysts making the change, and the timing. A penny cut to estimated earnings of $1 per share is minor during a stagnant

---

[3] *Aerospace Still Flying, Subprime Hitting Insurers*, Charles Rotblut, Zacks.com, February 13, 2008, www.zacks.com/commentary/6960/Aerospace+Still+Flying;+Subprime+Hitting+Insurers
[4] *Table from The Warnings Signs for Financials*, Charles Rotblut, Zacks.com, September 17, 2008, www.zacks.com/commentary/8615/The+Warning+Signs+For+Financials

economy, especially if most analysts are keeping their forecasts unchanged. A 5-cent positive revision to estimated earnings of 50 cents per share is significant, particularly if the majority of the covering analysts are changing their projections. As far as timing, the most recent changes should be more accurate because they reflect the most up-to-date information.

Also look at the company's recent record of earnings surprises. A 1% reduction to earnings may not be significant if a company has a track record of topping expectations. If the company has been missing expectations, any downward revision should be treated as a sign to get out of the stock.

I use earnings estimate revisions as a signal to do more research. I often find there is news related to the revision, whether it is updated guidance from the company or new industry data. In terms of timing, I use earnings estimate revisions to determine whether to buy a stock (rising earning estimates) or to hold off and keep an eye on the stock (falling earnings estimates).

Besides alerting me to potential news, there is a fundamental reason why earnings estimate revisions work. Valuation models, like Discounted Cash Flow[5], analyze a stock based on its future earnings potential. The higher future earnings are projected to be, the more the stock is worth. Therefore, positive revisions can drive a stock's price higher, whereas negative revisions cause it to fall.

Valuation

You should buy a stock for as low a valuation as possible. I will explain how to value a stock in chapters 8 and 9, but in terms of psychology, the explanation is simpler. Be prepared to sell a stock whose valuation has become excessive. A stock should not be commanding a high single-digit price-to-book (P/B) or a high double-digit price-to-earnings (P/E) multiple.

If you bought a stock that was trading at P/B multiple of 2.8 and a P/E multiple of 18, and now the stock is trading at a P/B multiple of 6.5 and P/E multiple of 60, consider selling it. Because the stock price has probably doubled, you should sell at least half your position. For the remainder of shares, use a trailing stop and monitor earnings estimate revisions. The stock could still trade higher, but make sure you have a plan to lock in the profits once the valuation becomes excessive. The potential risks outweigh the potential reward of continuing to hold onto the stock without a clear short-term sell strategy.

---

[5] See Chapter 9 for an explanation of Discounted Cash Flow.

News

News events are often the biggest reason to sell. The key is to monitor news releases for updates on business conditions, announcements impacting earnings, and unexpected events. What you are looking for is anything causing your opinion of the company to differ from your initial analysis.

Had you owned AIG in February 2008, the revelation of a potential $5 billion loss instead of a $1.6 billion loss would have been reason enough to sell. The loss of a major client is a reason to sell. Reduced earnings guidance is a reason to sell. Rumors of an accounting scandal are reasons to sell. The unexpected resignation of the CEO or CFO for "personal reasons" is a reason to sell.

If a merger is announced and you own shares in the company being acquired, consider selling all your position; particularly if the purchase price represents a significant premium to the pre-offer price. Mergers are highly unpredictable and can fall apart without much warning. This is why it is better to take a big profit before the merger deal is completed.

Conversely, if you own the acquiring company, then evaluate whether the merger makes sense and if the purchase price is too high. Also, consider management's past track record with mergers. Some companies are effective at making mergers work; Cisco Systems (CSCO) is a great example of this. Most others are not. In fact, cost savings from "synergies" are often not realized. So ask what the acquirer is getting from the merger; does it make good business sense and is the purchase price too high?

SOCIAL INVESTING

Social investing is making investment decisions based on your personal beliefs. If you are religious, you may not want to be associated with industries such as gambling or alcohol. If you are an environmentalist, you may not want to support companies that exploit natural resources. Perhaps you are a pacifist and do not like defense contractors. Or maybe you would rather put your money toward supporting companies that support social causes.

In the July/August 2009 issue of the *Financial Analysts Journal*, a study on social investing returns was published[6]. The authors found that "doing good while doing well" companies can outperform the market; one rationale

---

[6] *The Wages of Social Responsibility*, Meir Statman and Denys Glushkov, *Financial Analysts Journal*, July/August 2009, Vol. 65, No. 4: 33-46.

being such companies have better motivated employees (they feel better about the products they produce). These companies also benefit from a better public perception (e.g., no environmental scandals). Most socially responsible portfolios were found to be at a disadvantage, however, because they excluded stocks that might add to the overall returns.

Investing is a business decision designed to do only one thing: increase your wealth. Every group of companies you exclude narrows your choice of investment options. An economist will tell you to consider if maximizing your profit opportunities will allow you to support your personal causes over the long-term because there is a monetary and opportunity cost to social investing.

A moral and spiritual cost should also be considered. Though the goal of investing is to increase your wealth, it is not worth engaging in an activity that conflicts with your core beliefs. There is no single right way to balance your profit motivations with your personal values; you need to find the best mixture. This may mean a smaller group of investment options. Alternatively, it may mean maximizing profits to give more money to charity. You need to do what lets you sleep at night.

TECHNICAL ANALYSIS

Technical analysis, also known as "charting," uses historic prices and volume to predict future price movement. Technicians look at current and past trends to determine if a stock is likely to trade higher or lower. They also use these trends to determine buy-and-sell price targets.

The idea behind this analysis is that previous trends provide a good gauge of what the future will bring. If a certain pattern has resulted in an upward (or downward) price movement, it should do so in the future. The reality behind technical analysis is it only works because people believe it does. I have been called naïve for saying this, but the reality is there is nothing magical about a pendant, head and shoulders, golden cross or a cup and handle formation. Traders believe such patterns form an inflection point and they act accordingly.

As an investor, your job is not to question the validity behind technical analysis but to understand that many people use it. Having a basic understanding of technical analysis can limit the role emotions play in investing decisions. Technical analysis can be useful as long as you remember the biggest downfall of charting—a trend holds until it does not.

Notice how much this stock has fluctuated in price. It could continue to do so in the future. Chart reproduced with the permission of QuoteMedia. ©2010 Quotemedia.

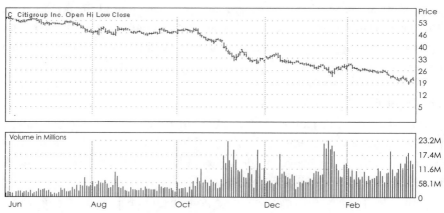

Notice the big drop in price between 2007 and 2008, a sign that Citigroup (C) was facing problems before the height of the credit crisis. Chart reproduced with the permission of QuoteMedia. ©2010 Quotemedia.

The best way to use charts is to identify events that affected the company, assess a stock's historic volatility, and analyze the risk level. All this can be accomplished with a basic understanding of technical analysis. Your goal is not to predict where the price could be headed over the next few days, but to identify potential situations that could cause you to lose money or make money. When used as a component of comprehensive stock analysis, charting can help.

I will show you a few stocks as examples of what to look for and how technical analysis can help you.

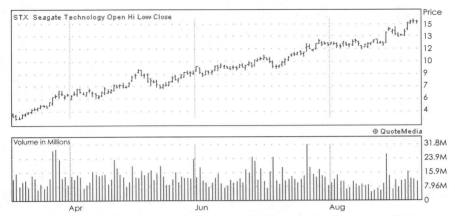

Business conditions started to improve, resulting in an upward trending price. Chart reproduced with the permission of QuoteMedia. ©2010 Quotemedia.

Price Trends

The most basic, and in some ways, important thing a chart can tell you is how a stock has traded. This can give you an idea of the stock's possible volatility and if the markets have a favorable or unfavorable attitude toward a stock. Sentiment can be an early sign that business conditions are good (upward trending chart) or bad (downward trending chart).

Past News Events

If you see a sudden spike or drop in the stock price, chances are some news was released. A big upward move could signal a positive earnings surprise, raised earnings guidance, the release of a new product or a merger. A big drop could signal an earnings miss, lowered profit guidance, the sudden departure of a key executive, an accounting scandal, a failed merger or other bad news. I am more concerned with the big price drops because I want to know what caused the decline and whether it was a one-time occurrence or something that may reoccur.

The chart on page 56 shows MultiFineline Electronix (MFLX), a circuit board and electronic components manufacturer. In January 2009, MFLX raised its earnings guidance, causing a jump in the stock price. About six weeks later, the company cut its guidance, citing uncertain business conditions. Notice the higher volume that accompanied both announcements. If your previous research had not unveiled anything, the two big price movements should prompt you to look at the news released around both dates.

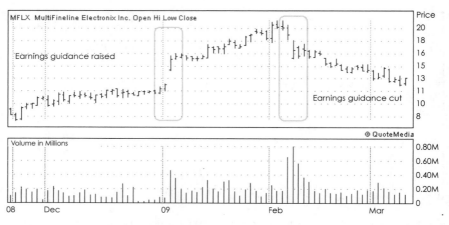

Chart reproduced with the permission of QuoteMedia. ©2010 Quotemedia.

HOW I ANALYZE CHARTS

Though I recognize the shortcomings of technical analysis, I view it as a good tool for assessing sentiment. It is a regular part of my analysis, but usually not the deciding factor. The exceptions are when a stock made a big run or I am concerned it could fall farther. When I am using a chart, I keep my assessment simple. Instead of looking for a complex pattern, I want to know if the stock is trending, if it is near support or resistance and whether the short-term sentiment is too bullish or bearish.

The chart of Texas Instruments on page 57 provides a good example of the analysis I use when looking at a chart.

1.   The top line is called "resistance." Notice how the stock has not traded above this level since July 2008. This indicates traders have been unwilling to pay more than $25 per share since then. The longer TXN stays below this level, the harder it will be for the stock to rise. A move above this line would be positive and is called a "breakout."

2.   The bottom line shows the lowest level the stock has traded at over the last two years. This is known as support, because it indicates investors believe the stock should not go much lower. Support can provide a good entry point as long as the stock bounces off the level, instead of falling below it. Make sure you understand the reason why a stock fell to a support level before buying it.

Chart reproduced with the permission of QuoteMedia. ©2010 Quotemedia.

3. The two trend lines are called "moving averages." They are actually a series of dots showing the average price for the previous 50 days (50-day moving average) and 200 days (200-day moving average). Moving average refers to the line tracing the average price for every day and moves up or down, depending on whether the average price is higher or lower. A moving average can identify a trend and tell you if a sentiment is bullish (the stock is above its moving average) or bearish (the stock is below its moving average). If a stock is trading significantly above its 50-day moving average, there may be too much optimism priced into it.

4. Volume can tell you several things about a stock. A spike in volume levels often means there was news; it can tell you if buying or selling was higher than normal on a given day. It can also tell you if the number of shares traded has decreased, a sign that investors are uncertain where the stock is trading next. I prefer stocks that average in excess of 100,000 shares traded per day because it will be easier to buy and sell. Furthermore, the higher the volume, the greater the number of people looking at the stock. A company can have a great story, but if nobody pays attention, the stock will have a harder time moving.

5. The Wilder RSI is designed to signal whether a stock is overbought (too much short-term optimism) or oversold (too much short-term pessimism). Notice the shaded peaks, they suggest the stock was overbought. In theory, this should mean the stock will pull back over the near-term. The problem with the Wilder RSI (and a similar indicator, stochastics) is that a stock can stay overbought or oversold for a period of time. Nonetheless, if the Wilder RSI is showing the stock to be overbought, be careful about buying it. If the stock is oversold, make sure you understand the cause of the pessimism.

KEY CHAPTER POINTS

1. Only do what allows you to sleep at night. If a stock or other investment keeps you up at night, sell it.
2. Keep a written journal of all your investments, including the reasons you bought a certain stock and what would cause you to sell it.
3. Use price limits to protect yourself from a large loss or to lock in a big gain.
4. Pay attention to changes in earnings estimate revisions. Sell a stock if profit projections are being cut.
5. There is a monetary and opportunity cost to social investing, but never engage in an activity contrary to your core beliefs.
6. Charts can identify events that have previously affected the company, assess a stock's historic volatility, and analyze the current risk level.

PART 2

Corporate Analysis:
How to Evaluate Business Models and Analyze Financial Statements

CHAPTER 4

Business Models

A business model is what a company does to make money. It may manufacture, fabricate, develop, provide, distribute, or sell various goods and services. How the company gets its customers to pay money is its business model.

Depending on the company, the model may be complex or simple. General Electric (GE) has multiple divisions focused on a variety of industries including health care, power generation, and finance. Gap (GPS), on the other hand, sells adult and children's clothing. The complexity or simplicity of the business model has little to do with a company's success. What matters is the size of the profit opportunity and if the company can take advantage of the opportunity. For instance, McDonald's (MCD) has stayed profitable for years by operating and franchising fast-food restaurants.

When evaluating a stock, one of the primary questions you should ask is "Do I know how the company makes money?" It may sound like a silly question, but it is critical to your investment decisions. After all, you cannot analyze what you do not understand. If you do not know what influences a company's sales trends, you will not be able to tell when conditions are likely to improve. Worse yet, you will not know what warning signs could indicate conditions are about to worsen, significantly increasing your risk.

Most investing websites post corporate profiles, making it easier to grasp a company's operations. Corporate press releases also provide basic descriptions. My favorite resource, however, is the 10-K. The 10-K is an annual report required by the SEC and is free and available online at http://www.sec.gov/edgar.shtml. This report provides a comprehensive description of a company's operations and often lists its primary customers and competitors.

Not all descriptions make sense. In fact, I have seen descriptions that do not explain what the company does or how it differs from its competitors. When this occurs, I look for another stock. If a company cannot explain what it does, it probably does not explain the benefits of its products and services to customers well, either. Who wants to own shares in a company that cannot sell its products? Not me.

There will also be businesses you do not understand, perhaps because of a business model's complexity or your lack of interest. Alternatively, you might grasp the concepts, but realize the factors influencing a company's success or failure are beyond your sphere of knowledge. There is nothing wrong with this; passing on such companies can enhance your returns by avoiding situations where you cannot assess the risk level.

On the other hand, understanding the business model does not make the company a good investment. For example, during the Internet bubble of the late 1990s, many dog and cat owners bought supplies and toys from *Pets.com*. The business model was straightforward; the company sold pet supplies online. However, the prices were too low for the company to make a profit and *Pets.com* shut down.

Not only is it important to understand the business model, but it is also important to determine if the company is capable of generating sustainable profits.

WHAT MAKES A BUSINESS MODEL WORK
A Need Must Be Fulfilled

The most important aspect of any business model is to fulfill a need. There has to be a reason why customers want to purchase the product. If there is no need, the product will not sell and profits will not be realized. For instance, a high-end French restaurant will struggle if it only targets low-income residents.

Most often the problem is not if there is demand, but if there is enough demand. Many businesses fail because they grow beyond the sustainable size of their markets. This is the case with product fads. Krispy Kreme (KKD) and Crocs (CROX) are examples of companies that grew beyond their sustainable markets.

What happens is sales start to rise rapidly, which attracts venture capitalists and other private equity firms sensing a profit opportunity. Money is invested, the company goes public, business expands from the influx of capital, more consumers are exposed to the product, the stock price rises, and early investors sell a large portion of their stake. At this point everyone is talking about the strength of the company's growth and the stock's performance. Then something happens and consumers spend their money elsewhere. Growth starts to slow (or even stop) and the stock price falls. At this point, a CEO has two options— either introduce a product to reinvigorate growth or scale down operations. Often neither happens; instead stories about mismanagement surface (e.g., accounting issues, inventory issues, disgruntled franchisees, angry customers) and the stock price drops even more.

Few companies cross the divide from having a successful product to having a line of successful products. This is why it is not a good idea to buy a stock because you like the company's product. There should be more reasons, particularly if the company is dependent on one or two key products. If demand for those products changes, the company will have problems. Also, just because you like the product does not mean other people do.

Need is relative to perception. There is no need to spend $200 on a pair of jeans, but many women think they look better in them. There is no need for a high-end sports car, but it is fun having one.

For other products, there is a real need. Consider Joy Global (JOYG), which makes mining equipment, such as high-end shovels. The global economy has an ever-increasing demand for basic materials such as metal and coal. Basic materials companies need to continue digging. Until we determine how to recycle waste and take no more metal or coal from the ground, there will be a need for mining equipment. The actual level of demand for Joy Global's equipment will fluctuate, but there will always be a need.

As an investor, you want to seek business models with a sustainable market. The market may not be as sustainable as mining, but there has to be a reason why the products continue to sell well. Drugs, semiconductors, laundry detergent, and farm equipment are examples of such products.

Be careful about products with a short lifespan in terms of popularity, the list of which is long. How do you know? A rule of thumb: be careful investing in any company dependent on one product experiencing a surge in popularity. Though there is money to be made if you invest early enough, the downside risks are huge.

The Product Must Be Profitable

Even if a company fulfills a need, it may not be profitable.

During the tech bubble of the 1990s, many companies received venture capital or conducted public offerings on the basis of their popularity. Among them were Drkoop.com and Pets.com. These, and many other companies, were delisted from the NASDAQ in 2001 because their stocks were trading below $1 per share.

As I write this book, *twitter* is one of the fastest growing companies on the Internet; it is attracting venture capitalists hoping to profit from its popularity. There is one problem, however; *twitter* generates no revenues, using it is free. At some point, the investors are hoping *twitter* starts to generate revenues. But whether those revenues will be enough to offset costs or if the method of generating revenues will cause users to go elsewhere is unknown. There is also the fad factor; the popularity of *twitter* could drop quickly as something else catches users' interests.

Though *twitter* may seem like an extreme example, it is no different than a biotech company with a promising new drug under development. For the company to achieve profitability, the drug has to be approved by regulatory agencies, added to insurance formularies, and prescribed by doctors instead of other competitive treatments. Just because a medication is brought to market does not mean it will sell enough to generate profits.

On the other hand, some companies are adept at making profitable products. Apple (AAPL) is a good example. The company expanded from making computers to mp3 players and mobile phones. It also operates the successful iTunes store, which sells music and videos, as well as third-party applications for the iPhone. What makes Apple so successful is not only that it knows how to design a product, but it also knows how to generate profitability for its products.

This is a key point—Apple understands both the importance of design and the ultimate goal of earning money.

Ten of thousands of companies have designed great products, but only a select few have figured how to turn products into a sustainable stream of profits. The lesson: it does not matter how much you like the product, if the company is not profitable, you should not invest in it.

Barriers to Entry Must Exist

A company needs a method of fending off competition, otherwise its profits will not be sustainable. The best way to accomplish this is barriers to entry. A barrier to entry is anything dissuading a would-be competitor from entering the market. It can be costs, patents, exclusive agreements, distribution, regulatory issues, the size of the market or access to resources. Without a barrier to entry, competitors will enter the market and drive down margins.

Barriers to entry differ by industry, but there are similarities. Coca-Cola (KO) has remained the most popular soft drink for decades because of its distribution agreements and its massive advertising budget. For a competitor to enter the soft-drink market, it would have to convince store owners to devote shelf space to its products, find a distribution system to get the drinks out, and fund advertising—none of which are cheap or easy.

There have been new entrants to the soft drink industry over the years. A stroll down the soda aisle of any grocery store will show how much shelf space is devoted to Coca-Cola products. More shelf space = more sales = more profits.

Costs play a big role in determining the amount of competition. It costs a relatively small amount to open a neighborhood restaurant, which is why so many fail or change owners. Conversely, Transocean (RIG), which operates offshore drilling rigs, is protected by the expense of entering its market. Major oil companies hire Transocean because the cost of buying and operating a rig is so expensive. At the same time, since the energy industry is cyclical, even if a potential competitor could afford to buy a rig, it would need the necessary capital resources to withstand periods of time when demand drops significantly.[1]

It is not only the cost of entering the market, but also the customer's cost of switching. The more difficult it is for a customer to switch to another vendor, the greater the barrier to entry. Oracle (ORCL) and SAP (SAP) are

---

[1] This was written before the explosion of the Transocean rig led to the oil spill in the Gulf of Mexico. An investor looking at Transocean would have to compare the potential liabilities against the barriers to entry that the company enjoys.

somewhat protected from competition because it is easier for a company to renew a license than to install a different software system. Not only is there the cost of contracting for the new software, but also costs assoicated with the labor to install the software, train employees, and re-create processes and reports previously run on the old system. It can be, and is done, but the process is not easy.

Acquisitions can be an effective means of creating an artificial barrier to entry. Cisco Systems (CSCO) acquires smaller technology companies. Though these purchases expand Cisco's product line and help the company adapt to a changing marketplace, the acquisitions make it difficult for would-be competitors to gain market share or steal current customers. Large pharmaceutical companies often acquire or enter into partnerships with smaller biotech companies to maintain control over new drugs.

A company does not have to be the market leader to have a barrier to entry, it only has to have a defensible market position. Alberto-Culver (ACV) has been profitable for years by selling beauty products. Alberto-Culver has developed a distribution system, maintains a sizeable amount of shelf space, and is well capitalized. All this helps the company maintain its competitive position.

WHAT CAUSES A BUSINESS MODEL TO FAIL?
Profits Are Not Realized
The biggest reason a business model fails is because the company cannot achieve profitability—more money is spent on operations than is brought in from sales. Most new businesses fail because they never achieve profitability.

Just because a company is traded on the New York Stock Exchange (NYSE) or the NASDAQ does not mean it is or will be profitable. People bought shares of *Pets.com* in February 2000, assuming the company would grow enough to be profitable. That never happened. *Pets.com's* access to additional funding was cut off and the company closed down because it could not finance its business operations. Many biotech companies suffer the same fate. The treatments in their pipeline never make it to market and funding for additional research is cut off.

Many new companies are unprofitable as they try to grow sales. The key is to determine if the losses are shrinking as sales are rising. Even if the losses are shrinking, shareholders still have to contend with dilutive measures, such as secondary stock offerings or convertible debt financing. Both of these measures result in current shareholders seeing their stake in the company reduced, meaning their stake is worth less than before. A one-time secondary offering could prove to be a savvy business move, but if the company has to continuously raise capital to fund business operations, the business model is flawed.

Failure to Adapt to Change

No matter how profitable the current business model, a company will not stay profitable if it does not respond to change. Industry conditions, consumer tastes, and technological innovations can make a previously sound business model out-dated. The requirement for management is to identify changing trends as they develop and respond to them rapidly and correctly. Failure to do so can have damaging effects.

The impact of not responding to change is evident in the newspaper industry. Prior to the birth of the web, newspapers made considerable money from advertising, particularly classified advertisements. The first large-scale threat to this was the birth of online auction facilitator *eBay* (EBAY) and employment website *Monster.com* (MWW). Both sites offered direct competition to the most profitable portion of the newspaper's business model. Several years later, *craigslist* dealt an additional blow by providing free online advertising[2].

In both instances, rather than move to thwart or acquire these companies, newspaper publishers allowed the competition to grow and prosper. The newspaper industry had the customer base to act aggressively against these threats, but it failed to do so.

Similarly, U.S. automakers struggled because of their inability to predict and respond to changing energy prices. The oil embargos of the 1970s allowed Japanese carmakers Toyota (TM) and Honda (HMC) to make inroads into the United States with small, more fuel-efficient vehicles. Chrysler, Ford (F), and General Motors were caught off-guard and struggled to catch up with competitive vehicles. In 2007 and 2008, history repeated itself when oil prices skyrocketed again. The focus of the American car companies had been on SUVs, while Toyota and Honda manufactured hybrid cars and fuel-efficient cars consumers really wanted.

---

[2] Though *craigslist* is private and does not provide any financial information, the company could be profitable. In 2008, consulting firm Classified Intelligence issued a press release estimating *craigslist* generated $81 million in revenues from the small group of categories it does charge for.

Inability to Maintain Customer Loyalty

Though product loyalty has helped Coca-Cola throughout the years, it can also be the weakest of all barriers to entry. The easier it is for a consumer (whether an individual or a business) to switch to a competitor, the tougher it will be to maintain profitability.

Consider what has happened to Internet search engines. Yahoo (YHOO) was the dominant search engine until web users decided they liked Google (GOOG) better. Numerous other search engines also failed, such as Northern Light, Excite, and Lycos, because the cost of switching a search engine is only a matter of typing in a different web address.

Product loyalty becomes important when the company is dependent on one or two items to drive sales. If popularity wanes, business suffers. Crocs has had little success expanding beyond its rubber clogs and sales have suffered as a result. Motorola (MOT) lost considerable market share in the mobile phone market when it failed to build on the success of its RAZR cell phone. Though the phone was the best-selling mobile device in history, new products from Apple and other companies swayed consumers from Motorola. Consumers did not see the value in staying with Motorola when other companies were offering what seemed to be better devices.

If the product driving sales represents a fad, such as rubber clogs, instead of fulfilling a need, such as offshore drilling rigs, the riskier a business model becomes. This raises the risk of investing, especially if the company cannot expand its product line. The only way to invest in such companies is early in the product cycle with a clear plan to get out before popularity peaks. It is better to miss out on the opportunity than to invest when the product is nearing its peak. How do you know when it peaks? If the valuation seems high and there is a lot of talk about the company's strong growth, it is probably too late to buy the stock.

Too Much Competition

Even in industries where barriers to entry exist, there can be too much competition. When this occurs, profit margins are squeezed and it is difficult for any company to make profits on a sustained basis.

The best example is the airline industry. Though significant barriers do exist, there is too much competition. The primary criterion for choosing an airline is the company with the cheapest flight at a specific time and destination. There is little difference in flying coach between one airline and another. Given this lack of differentiation, travelers go with the cheapest flight working with their schedule. (Yes, frequent flyer miles do play a role, but they are secondary to cost. This is evident in the development of many specialized travel search engines, such as SideStep and KAYAK.)

The combination of too much competition and low cost of switching from one vendor to another is damaging. In the technology sector this can be seen in the profit margins for contract manufacturers, such as Sanmina-SCI (SANM).

Sanmina-SCI and its competitors are hired by other companies to manufacturer electronic products. Technology companies design and sell products while relying on contract manufacturers such as Sanmina-SCI to handle the capital intensive work of making the product. Because most of the intellectual property is owned by the customer (e.g., technology companies), the contract manufacturers are forced to compete on price and quality of work, which results in low margins. During the past five years, Sanmina-SCI has lost money on an operating basis more often than it has made money.

Competition can also form if barriers to entry are low. This occurs when a company unveils a new product or finds a new niche. If profits prove (or are believed to become) substantial, competitors will enter the market, driving down prices. The camera market was once dominated by Nikon, Cannon, Olympus, and Pentax. Now, Sony (SNE) and Casio digital cameras are easy to find at many stores. Similarly, many companies manufacture mp3 players. Though Apple continues to be market leader, competition for non-iPod devices is fierce. This is why Microsoft (MSFT), despite all its capital resources, has failed to make significant headway with its Zune mp3 player. Flat panel television makers are also being challenged by competition. In all three cases the technology required to create the devices is well known among companies, making it easier to bring competitive products to market.

THE IMPACT OF BUSINESS CYCLES

Nearly all companies will be affected by periodic changes in business conditions. The growth rates of some companies are directly tied to economic cycles with business doing better during times of expansion and worse during recessions, hence the term "cyclicals." Other companies are tied to commodity prices. Still others are exposed to product upgrade cycles or patent expirations. Knowing what historic trends affect the company and identifying where it is in the cycle can determine if it is time to buy or sell the stock. Even over the course of a year, companies can experience good and bad business cycles.

The biggest influence by far will be the economy. If consumers are cutting back on their spending, business will slow across the board. A drop in consumer spending not only hurts retailers, but causes manufacturing to slow (fewer goods being produced) and transportation revenues to fall (fewer goods being shipped). An increase in unemployment will also affect banks (higher level of defaults) and housing (fewer potential buyers). The ripple effect can be seen in the commodity markets with lower demand for metals (factories buy less) and oil (fewer workers commuting to work and taking vacations). On the other hand, if the economy expands, consumer spending picks up, creating greater demand for a variety of other businesses. Corporations need consumers to consume products or business does not grow overall.

Product cycles add an additional level of volatility for certain industries. The lifespan for PCs and servers is estimated to be three to four years. Combined with the introduction of new operating systems, this creates a cyclical swing in demand. The ripple effect goes beyond PCs and servers, but can effect spending on semiconductors, storage devices, and software. The video gaming industry is also subject to product cycles. The introduction of next-generation gaming systems generates an increase in sales for new devices and new games. As the systems age, sales drop.

Drug companies are affected by patent expirations. Once a patent expires, competitors are allowed to sell competitive, generic versions. For a company relying on a few blockbuster drugs, patent expiration can have a significant negative impact on revenues and profits. As a result, some drug stocks will lag in the market a couple years before expiration if investors do not believe the company has new drugs capable of offsetting the loss of revenues.

Fortunately for investors, there is information published online that makes it easier to assess a company's place in a business cycle. Economic reports for nearly all data points are released on a weekly and monthly basis. (There are also calendars indicating what data will be released during the current week.) Many industry associations and consulting firms also publish data or press releases covering the main points. Though some industry associations try to pitch an optimistic tone (the National Association of Realtors is known for this), the data can provide useful insights. There are a number of blogs putting data into the context of the broader trends. A sheet of paper with the monthly numbers written down can also provide an understanding of how the trends develop over time.

BUY AN INDUSTRY LEADER OR NOT?

A school of thought suggests investors should focus on buying the leaders in each industry because they are in the best position to protect profits and fend off competition. While I do not disagree with this rationale, industry leaders often trade at premium valuations.

A company not leading in its industry can provide better returns. The key is operating with barriers to entry and in an industry segment with little competition, while trading at an attractive valuation. The upside of such companies is they may eventually become acquisition targets. The downside is a bigger competitor could decide to compete against them. While I would not ignore industry leaders, I would not pass on their smaller competitors.

KEY CHAPTER POINTS

1. Understand how a company makes money before investing in it.
2. Successful companies sell products that fulfill needs, are profitable, and enjoy barriers to entry.
3. Companies fail because they cannot achieve sustainable profitability, do not respond to change, fail to maintain customer loyalty or operate in markets without significant barriers to entry.
4. Know what trends affect a company's business cycle and where the company is in the current business cycle.
5. A company that is not an industry leader can be a profitable investment.

CHAPTER 5

The Balance Sheet

Introduction to Financial Statement Analysis

The next three chapters discuss how to analyze the balance sheet, the income statement, and the cash flow statements. Each chapter contains both a components section and quick analysis section. The components section provides an explanation of the line items found on financial statements. The quick analysis section discusses how to evaluate these three statements. If you have a strong accounting background, you may want to skip to the quick analysis section.

The presentation of the financial statements can vary from website to website. To help analyze the numbers, regardless of presentation, I have restricted my descriptions to the most commonly seen line items. In addition, I also have listed commonly used alternate names.

Occasionally, data will be notated as being "restated" or "reclassified." Restated means the numbers changed since the company first released results for the specific quarter or year. This often reflects a change in a business division, a divesture or a shift in accounting policy. Reclassified means certain expenses (or income) were shifted from one line item to another. In both instances, especially if the changes were made for more than one year, it helps to understand why the change was made.

The balance sheet is a listing of the company's assets and liabilities. It is unique among financial metrics because it is a snapshot of one day in the company's fiscal year rather than a running account of how business is doing.

A good way to understand a balance sheet is to consider your own financial situation. You have various assets: checking account, savings account, cars, a house, stocks, 401K, collectibles, furniture, etc. All of these have value. Some are short-term (i.e., "current")—such as the money in your wallet, whereas others are long-term—like fine jewelry. If you were to add the value of everything you possess, you would have the value of your assets.

You also have various liabilities. Some of them are short-term obligations, such as your electricity bill or taxes. Other loans are long-term, such as your mortgage. You might also have upcoming obligations like college tuition or a wedding.

Ideally, the total value of your assets exceeds those of your liabilities. If so, the difference is your net worth. If you were a business, we would call the amount by which your assets exceeds your liabilities "equity."

As an example, say you calculated your net worth on a Friday. Feeling good about your net worth, you go out to a nice restaurant and a play on Saturday. On Sunday, you buy groceries. If you recalculated your net worth on Monday, would it be the same as it was on Friday?

Of course not. You spent money over the weekend. Either the cash is gone or you have a new balance on your credit card (a note payable). You might have also accumulated credit points (a deferred asset).

A company is no different. On any given day, it has supplies to buy, inventories to replenish, and invoices to pay. Additionally, it is receiving both revenues and orders from customers. As a result, the balance sheet published on the last day of the quarter will have different numbers than a balance sheet created a day, a week or a month later.

A balance sheet is a snapshot of a company's financial condition at a certain time. Over a period of quarters and years, trends emerge that can either be favorable or unfavorable. Even from one quarter to the next, changes in the balance sheet can raise questions.

For instance, if inventory showed a significant increase, you would want to know why. It could be a good thing—a big order got placed right at the end of the quarter—or a bad thing—products are not selling.

By analyzing the balance sheet you get a sense of the company's finances and quickly know if something needs to be questioned.

Before I discuss the primary line items, I will explain why it is called a balance sheet. The term refers to the pre-computer days when assets and liabilities were kept in separate books. Accountants had to reconcile the two books to make sure they matched, or balanced.

The balance sheet shows the assets (top) and the liabilities and equity (bottom). At all times, total assets must match the total liabilities and equity. In other words, assets must "balance" liabilities and equity. (You never have to worry about the balance sheet being out of whack, because it is the accountant's job to make sure everything lines up.)

Let us get into the details of the balance sheet and what you should know about each of the primary line items.

ASSETS

The Table below shows Caterpillar's (CAT) assets.

PERIOD ENDING	31-Dec-08	31-Dec-07	31-Dec-06
Assets			
Current Assets			
Cash And Cash Equivalents	2,736,000	1,122,000	779,000
Short Term Investments	-	-	-
Net Receivables	19,351,000	16,568,000	15,705,000
Inventory	8,781,000	7,204,000	6,351,000
Other Current Assets	765,000	583,000	258,000
Total Current Assets	**31,633,000**	**25,477,000**	**23,093,000**
Long Term Investments	15,837,000	14,745,000	14,018,000
Property Plant and Equipment	12,524,000	9,997,000	8,851,000
Goodwill	2,261,000	1,963,000	1,904,000
Intangible Assets	511,000	475,000	387,000
Accumulated Amortization	-	-	-
Other Assets	1,705,000	3,475,000	677,000
Deferred Long Term Asset Charges	3,311,000	-	1,949,000
Total Assets	**67,782,000**	**56,132,000**	**50,879,000**

Current Assets
Current assets are assets that are highly liquid (e.g. cash) or are intended to be used within the course of a year.

Cash & Cash Equivalents
The first line item you will see on a balance sheet is cash & cash equivalents. Cash is self-explanatory; it is an accounting of how much money the company has in

its bank accounts, registers, safes, etc. These include cash and cash equivalents, short-term investments, accounts receivable, inventory, prepaid expenses, and other current assets

Cash equivalents is money invested in highly liquid assets for use within a 90-day period; this typically includes money market accounts, CDs, short-term treasury bills, etc. Companies sit on millions (and for some, billions) of dollars in cash so it only makes sense they try to earn some interest.

Short-term Investments

On some balance sheets, a line item for short-term investments or marketable securities will appear. These are stocks, bonds, and warrants the company intends to sell over the next 12 months. They usually reflect management's effort to earn extra income while maintaining easily accessible funds.

Short-term marketable securities are listed at their current price, not the price at which the asset was purchased. For example, if management bought $500,000 worth of shares in XYZ and the stock drops 10%, the investment would be listed as being worth $450,000 on the balance sheet, with the $50,000 loss being counted against income.

Accounts Receivable

Sometimes referred to as receivables, this is how much money customers owe the company. A receivable is recorded when a sale is made and the customer uses credit to pay for the transaction; this means the seller expects to be paid during the next 30 to 90 days.

Under accounts receivable, you might see a line item called doubtful accounts or something similar. This is an accounting of how much money the company believes it will not collect. In other words, the seller is owed money, but the customer refuses to pay. Net receivables include any deduction for doubtful accounts.

These are items to pay attention to because they can alert you that something is not right with the business. An unexplained drop in accounts receivables means the customers are not placing orders or more customers are paying in cash.

Notes Receivable – Short-term

If a company extends credit or otherwise makes a short-term loan, it will appear as a note receivable. The difference between an account receivable and a note receivable is an account receivable is for a bill of sale, whereas a note receivable is a loan.

When a customer is involved, a note receivable is recorded if the customer is paying a bill on an installment plan or otherwise paying interest. Note receivables can also be loans to employees or other entities, such as a supplier. These loans are only as good as the borrowers' ability to pay.

Inventory

Mention inventories and most people have visions of warehouses stacked with products. This line item shows the value of those products, plus everything needed to create and package them. Any physical item related to the production or packaging of a product is counted as inventory.

Sometimes, inventory is followed by a sub-item labeled "raw materials." Raw materials are the basic items used to make a product. For example, Ball Corporation (BLL) makes metal cans and other containers. It breaks down inventories as "raw materials and supplies" and "Work-in-process and finished goods." Raw materials are the metal and other materials it needs to make the products; work-in-progress are items in production but not finished. Remember, the balance sheet is a snapshot of a certain day, so if an unfinished can is sitting on a production line, it is still counted as inventory. Because the can is not finished, it is considered a work-in-progress. Finished goods are any product ready to be shipped, but not yet delivered.

Prepaid Expenses

Prepaid expenses are expenses paid for in advance. These are often reoccurring costs, such as insurance.

Other Current Assets

This is a big category for any assets expected to be used or sold within the next 12 months that do not fit into the aforementioned categories. As long as they are not of significant size, they are not of much concern. Like any other asset, though, they could hurt earnings if they need to be devalued at some point.

Total Current Assets

The total value of cash & cash equivalents, short-term investments, accounts receivable, notes receivable—short-term, inventory, prepaid expenses, and other current assets.

LONG-TERM ASSETS

Long-term assets are assets intended to be kept for periods of more than 12 months. These include property, plant and equipment, goodwill, intangibles, long-term investments, long-term notes receivable, and other long-term assets.

Property, Plant & Equipment

Also referred to as fixed assets, these are the tangible assets required to run a business. Included in this are buildings, machines, land, furniture, computers, vehicles, etc. Assets acquired through capital leases are also listed here.

Often depreciation and net property, and plant and equipment are shown. Depreciation is how much the assets have decreased in value. Companies are allowed to deduct a certain amount every year to account for an asset worth less now than it was 12 months ago. The rate of depreciation varies by the asset, with computers losing their value quickly and buildings depreciated over a lengthy period of time. As I will explain in the next chapter, depreciation is a non-cash charge against income.

The key point to remember is after an item is fully depreciated, it still has some value. For example, a five-year old printer may have no value on the balance sheet, but at an auction, it could sell for a price above zero dollars.

Goodwill

Sometimes included as part of intangibles, goodwill is the premium paid for acquiring another company. It is any amount in excess of the underlying value of the net assets.

For example, a company buys a bakery. Goodwill would be any amount paid in excess of the value of the ovens, baking pans, flour, etc. This premium would be warranted if the recipes or brand name had special value. Depending on the presentation of the balance sheet, goodwill may be grouped with intangibles.

Intangibles

Intangibles are non-physical assets that a company believes has value. Trademarks, patents, logos, web domain names, and recipes all fall under this category. The value of an intangible asset is subjective and it is not uncommon for a company to overestimate the true value of an intangible asset, particularly when a merger occurs. To be fair, some intangible assets do have significant value, such as the recipe for Coca-Cola. Other intangibles, such as patents, can be practically worthless.

Intangible assets are assumed to lose value over time. This deterioration of value is accounted through amortization. This is a non-cash charge a company incurs.

Long-term Investments

Investments intended to be held for longer than 12 months are long-term investments. They often represent an equity or debt investment in another firm. A company would do this to have access to new products or maintain a close relationship.

Notes Receivable—Long-term

This is the portion of loans made by the company not expected to be paid within the next 12 months. Again, these loans are only as good as the borrowers' ability to pay.

Other Long-term Assets

This is for any long-term asset not fitting under the other categories. Deferred charges may be grouped here or listed as a separate line item. Deferred charges occur when a company has a big upfront expense, but receives benefit from the expenditure over a lengthy period of time. Accounting rules allow the firm to spread the cost over time. An example is if a company spends money rearranging its facilities to improve production. There would be a large upfront cost, but the benefits would be realized over time. The company is allowed to spread the expenses over several quarters or years, instead of incurring a large charge against earnings in one particular quarter. (Deferred taxes may also be listed here or as a separate line item.)

Deferred charges have no cash value and in the event of liquidation, would be deemed worthless. They are purely a paper asset.

Deposits & Other Assets

This can also be used for any long-term asset that does not fit under the other categories. It can consist of long-term deposits, long-term debts owed to the company, prepaid bills, etc.

Total Assets

Total assets are the sum of all current and long-term assets. If you think of a balance sheet as split between a left and right column, the left side would be assets and the right side would be liabilities and equity. Total assets must equal the sum of debt and equity. Hence the sheet is balanced.

LIABILITIES

The Table below shows Caterpillar's (CAT) liabilities.

Liabilities			
Current Liabilities			
Accounts Payable	12,341,000	10,694,000	9,636,000
Short/Current Long Term Debt	12,701,000	10,600,000	9,616,000
Other Current Liabilities	1,027,000	951,000	-
Total Current Liabilities	**26,069,000**	**22,245,000**	**19,252,000**
Long Term Debt	22,834,000	17,829,000	17,680,000
Other Liabilities	12,268,000	7.175.000	5,879,000
Deferred Long Term Liability Charges	-	-	1,209,000
Minority Interest	524,000	-	-
Negative Goodwill	-	-	-
Total Assets	**67,782,000**	**56,132,000**	**50,879,000**

Current Liabilities

Current liabilities are amounts owed that need to be paid within a year. They normally include accounts payable, accrued expenses, notes payable, the current portion of long-term debt, and capital leases and other current liabilities.

Accounts Payable

This is money the company owes to its vendors. It is the exact opposite of accounts receivable. A company records an account payable when it is billed for a product or raw material purchased for normal business operations.

An unexplained increase in accounts payables could signal the company is having problems paying its bills. You can monitor this by calculating accounts payable turnover, which is cost of goods sold divided by accounts payable. (A more accurate calculation is purchases made on credit divided by accounts payable. The purchases data is more difficult to find, however, and is not necessarily for most investors.)

Accrued Expenses

These are expenses the company will have to pay within the next 12 months, but are not due as of the date of the balance sheet. An example would be if the company contracted for a six-month project, with payment due at completion. Each month, the company would record an amount equal to one-sixth the total bill, listing the liability as an accrued expense. In other words, the company is creating a budget entry every month for a bill they will soon owe.

Notes Payable

Notes payable are short-term loans made to the company. Most often, a company will tap a line of credit or other type of short-term loan to pay for raw materials or business expenses. Doing so provides the company more flexibility for managing its cash.

These are not problematic unless there is a big increase in a single quarter or a disproportionate rise over a few quarters. If that happens, questions need to be asked. It could involve the timing of certain orders or signal the company is having fiscal problems.

Current Portion of Long-Term Debt and Capital Leases

Long-term debt consists of loans scheduled to be paid over more than 12 months. For publicly-traded companies, this usually consists of bonds, though a company can borrow from banks or other lenders.

Capital leases can be used to acquire machinery, a building or other fixed asset. It may be more advantageous for a company to use a capital lease than purchase a fixed asset.

Because capital leases last over several years, the amount owed is split between the current (due within 12 months) and long-term liabilities.

If a company has long-term debt or uses capital leases, it will divide the liabilities into current portion and long-term. The difference is when payments are due. Payments due within the next 12 months are current and are listed on the top half of the liabilities section. The remainder of the balance is listed on the bottom half.

Problems arise when a large liability is due within the next 12 months relative to cash and receivables and the company does not have access to financing or other capital. Be wary if you see a large increase in the current portion of long-term debt because most companies will either pay down the debt or refinance before a significant portion becomes due.

Other Current Liabilities

This is a collection of all liabilities due within the next 12 months, but not listed elsewhere. (An example would be taxes.) If the amount is proportionately small, then there is not much need for analysis. However, if it is a sizable portion of current liabilities, do more research. Details about what is included should be listed in the company's annual report filing with the SEC, which is referred to as the 10-K. It may be a bond due, or it could be something questionable.

Total Current Liabilities

This is the sum of the aforementioned line items. For fiscally sound companies, it will always be less than total current assets.

LONG-TERM LIABILITIES

Long-term liabilities are loans due in more than 12 months. They include long-term debt, non-current capital leases, deferred income tax, deferred income, minority interest, and other long-term liabilities.

Long-Term Debt

These are loans, primarily bonds, which are due in more than 12 months. As a rule of thumb, the more capital intensive a business is, the more long-term debt it will have. (In other words, a manufacturer will have more long-term debt than a software company.) It may also be advantageous from a tax standpoint to use debt to pay for expansion, equipment upgrades, and other related activities.

When looking at long-term debt, consider the type of company and determine what the debt has been for. As long as debt levels are manageable and the money has been used for a good purpose, it is okay to report long-term debt.

Non-Current Capital Leases

This is the portion of capital lease obligations due in more than 12 months. As long as the debt is manageable, capital obligations are not a problem.

Deferred Income Tax

A deferred tax liability arises when there is a difference between what the company reports to taxing authorities and what it reports to shareholders. This may sound dishonest, but it is not. Rather, a deferred tax liability is a product of accounting rules. Companies can use aggressive depreciation methods to lower the amount they pay in taxes. However, generally accepted accounting principles (GAAP) may require a different depreciation calculation be used. This difference results in a deferred tax.

Confusing? This is why CPAs can be well paid. Here is an example to show how a deferred tax liability can occur.

A company has a profitable year and uses some of its money to buy new equipment. Since it is facing a large tax bill, it decides to use an accelerated depreciation schedule to report as large an expense as possible. (This method allows the company to report a disproportionately large depreciation expense in Year 1 and smaller expenses in the years to follow.) But the company also knows the new equipment will yield benefits for several years, so it uses straight-line depreciation (the same depreciation expense is recorded every year) when reporting to shareholders. The latter method gives a more accurate account of operating expenses.

The difference between the two calculations is recorded as a deferred tax liability. As the years pass, the liability begins to disappear. Keep in mind this is a non-cash liability, meaning it does not have to be paid back. It is worth looking at the footnotes to see what the deferred tax is, but otherwise, it should not have a significant bearing on your analysis.

Minority Interest

When a company owns or holds less than a 100% stake in a subsidiary, the amount not owned by the company is a minority interest. For example, say the parent firm acquires an 80% interest in a subsidiary, but the original owner of the subsidiary still holds a 20% stake. The 20% stake is recorded on the balance sheet as a minority interest.

Minority interest is not a liability because the parent company is not obligated to repay the balance. However, it is not an asset owned by the parent company either. Therefore, it is a hybrid line item that lacks a proper place on the balance sheet. While many firms will report minority interest as part of liabilities, others may display it as a separate line item or list it at the top of the shareholder's equity section. When analyzing liabilities, it is best to exclude minority interest.

Deferred Income

Deferred income is money received for a service or product yet to be delivered. This can occur when a supplier bills a customer before goods are delivered. Technically the supplier owes the customer a benefit, whether it is consulting or a physical product. A liability is created because the work has not been completed. Though this line item is a function of accounting rules, the supplier can be sued for the amount if it fails to make good on its obligations.

Other Long-Term Liabilities

These are long-term debts not classified elsewhere. They can include deferred income (money received for a service or product that will not be delivered within the next 12 months), pension benefits, retiree health benefits, settlements to lawsuits, notes payable to third-parties, etc. Depending on the presentation of the balance sheet, mortgages could be included here or listed as a separate line item.

If the amount listed is significant, investigate the debt and ask questions if the amount of non-current liabilities suddenly rises.

Total Liabilities

Total liabilities are the total amount owed by the company; current liabilities plus long-term liabilities.

SHAREHOLDER'S EQUITY

In theory, shareholders can lay claim to any amount not owed by the company. However, accounting rules do not make the math that simple. As a result, you will see this section divided into preferred stock, common stock, additional paid-in capital, retained earnings, treasury stock, other equity, and total shareholders' equity.

The Table below shows Caterpillar's (CAT) shareholder's equity.

Stockholders' Equity			
Misc Stocks Options Warrants	-	-	-
Redeemable Preferred Stock	-	-	-
Preferred Stock	-	-	-
Common Stock	3,057,000	2,744,000	2,465,000
Retained Earnings	19,826,000	17,398,000	14,593,000
Treasury Stock	(11,217,000)	(9,451,000)	(7,352,000)
Capital Surplus	-	-	-
Other Stockholder Equity	(5,579,000)	(1,808,000)	(2,847,000)
Total Stockholder Equity	6,087,000	8,883,000	6,859,000
Net Tangible Assets	$3,315,000	$6.445.000	$4,568,000

Preferred Stock

This is a hybrid security some companies sell to raise capital. Preferred stock pays a regular dividend that is most often higher than what common shares yield. "Preferred" means preferred shareholders are entitled to receive their dividends before common shareholders do.

Despite the name, preferred stock has plenty of risks. The dividend is dependent on the company's ability to generate income. Preferred shareholders have limited voting power. In a bankruptcy scenario, bond holders receive priority over preferred shareholders. Though preferred shareholders do have priority over common shareholders to any remaining assets, there typically are no assets.

Common Stock

For common shares, par value is meaningless. It is a value assigned to each share according to the corporate charter. Depending on the state of incorporation, a company may be required to maintain that amount in equity. Therefore, most companies assign a very low par value to stocks, often a penny per share.

Additional Paid-in Capital

All stock offerings for publicly-traded companies are conducted at a price above par, so the difference between offer price and par needs to be accounted for. This

increase of stock price over par

amount is listed as additional paid-in capital or capital surplus. For example, if an offering priced the stock at $20 per share and the par value was listed as a penny, $19.99 for each share sold would be listed as capital surplus.

Retained Earnings

As a company earns money, any amount not paid out through dividends will go back into funding business operations, or be retained. Therefore, retained earnings are net income minus dividends paid. Common shareholders lay claim to all earnings not paid out to preferred shareholders; this amount is recorded in the balance sheet's equity section.

Treasury Stock

When a company repurchases outstanding shares, the amount paid for those shares is listed as treasury stock. Once the stock is repurchased, the company can either hold onto the shares or retire them. A company may not retire the shares if it is has an employee stock option program.

Because the company paid cash to acquire the shares, treasury stock is shown as a negative on the balance sheet. The company used shareholders' money to buy back stock, reducing the amount of assets to which shareholders have claim.

Other Equity

This frequently reflects changes in foreign currency and the value of non-current investments.

Total Shareholders' Equity

Total shareholders' equity is the sum of preferred stock, common stock, capital surplus, retained earnings, other equity, and treasury stock.

Total Liabilities & Shareholder's Equity

This is the sum of all liabilities and equity. For the balance sheets to balance, this total must equal the value of all assets.

QUICK ANALYSIS: THE BALANCE SHEET

In general, shareholders want a company to have a lot of cash and equity. In reality, the amount of cash, inventory, fixed assets, intangible assets, and debt will vary based on the industry in which the company operates. Companies that produce physical assets, such as manufacturers and fabricators, will have higher inventory, fixed assets, and liabilities than companies that provide more intangible assets, such as software or consulting firms.

For example, Caterpillar (CAT) makes various types of machines. It needs metal and factories—neither of which is cheap. It is considered to be capital-intensive, meaning a lot of cash is needed to operate the business. In contrast, Microsoft (MSFT) creates software. The capital required to provide one additional software license is nominal, because raw materials and factories are not required. Therefore, Microsoft is not considered to be a capital-intensive business.

Investors should consider the industry a company operates in and compare its balance sheet to its peers, as opposed to companies with which it has little in common.

The biggest rule when looking at a balance sheet is to question any large changes. A big change in a particular line item may be for a valid reason (e.g., the company built up inventory in anticipation of a product launch). Sometimes there is not a valid reason, which is a sign a problem could exist.

To help you identify potential problems or positive changes, here are a few of things you need to look at.

Cash

Cash is a double-edge sword. If a business has too little cash, it will not be able to function. If a company has too much cash, earnings will suffer. Worse yet, management may use the cash to pursue projects not benefitting shareholders.

A good example is Microsoft, which had $8.8 billion in cash and cash equivalents at the end of its fiscal 2010 first quarter. The company's investment in Internet properties and the Xbox gaming system have provided questionable results for shareholders.

What is the right amount of cash? There is no simple answer because needs vary from company to company. A manufacturing company requires more access to cash than a software company. Similarly, a company experiencing strong growth will require more cash than an industry peer that is established and stable.

Notes Receivable

For publicly traded companies, notes receivables are usually not of significant size. But if they account for more than 5% of current assets, investigate. It could be a one-time loan or something else. In particular, be wary of companies making large loans to their executives. This could be a way of providing extra compensation, even though doing so does not benefit shareholders.

Inventory

A company, in conjunction with its accountants, decides the value of the inventory. The price paid is used for the value of the raw materials, but once production is started, the value changes. A piece of wood might be worth one amount, but as soon as it is fabricated into a table, it is worth more. Therefore investors have to take a leap of faith in trusting the inventory's value.

Counterbalancing this leap of faith should be an understanding of the company's business model, the competitive landscape, and the products' life cycles. A product that customers are not buying may be worth far less than the cost of the raw materials. Raw materials can fluctuate in value depending on the commodity markets. A hot new product may actually be worth more than the stated value if demand outweighs supply.

The biggest risk is a company, and/or its competitors, will have too much supply, creating downward pressure on prices. This happened in 2008 with semiconductor companies. Chipmakers fabricated too much flash memory, driving down prices. This was great for consumers, but it devalued the chips sitting in the companies' warehouses. Similarly, new homebuilders found themselves taking losses on the value of houses and land contracts in 2008 and 2009 when buyers disappeared.

Intangibles

As noted earlier, the value assigned to intangibles is subjective. If intangibles account for a significant portion of total assets, then shareholders equity could be overstated. When assessing price-to-book (see Chapter 9), it may be useful to omit intangibles from the equation to accurately assess the company's true valuation.

Long-Term Debt

Like cash, long-term debt is a double-edged sword.

If a company needs additional capital to build a new factory or fund an acquisition, it makes sense to take on additional debt. Tax deductions are often a consideration; raising new debt does not dilute current shareholders' equity stake, whereas a secondary stock offering would.

On the other hand, the company must pay the debt back with interest. This hurts future earnings and may limit the company's ability to fund future projects at favorable rates. Furthermore, rules placed by the bond holders (i.e., debt covenants) could create problems should business conditions deteriorate. Most importantly, bond holders have priority over shareholders in the event of a bankruptcy and can force liquidation.

RATIOS

There are five key ratios to assess the strength or weakness of a company's balance sheet.

Current Ratio

Total current assets divided by total current liabilities.

The current ratio is a measure of a company's liquidity or how it meets its current obligations. This ratio should always be above 1.0. Ratios above 2.0 may signal the company has a significant amount of cash or inventory. If the reason is a large cash balance and the company is well-managed, a high current ratio is acceptable. Conversely, if the current ratio reflects a high level of accounts receivables or inventory, analyze the receivables or inventory turnover ratio. (I will explain how shortly).

Quick Ratio

Total current assets, less inventories, divided by total current liabilities.

Also known as the acid test, this ratio shows if a company can meet its obligations with accessible cash. Accounts receivable are included because a company can either collect invoices faster or sell invoices to a third party (a process known as factoring). The ratio omits inventories because stockpiles may not be easily sold.

Higher numbers are better, especially values above 1.0. But a capital-intensive firm may not have a quick ratio above 1.0.

Debt/Equity

Total liabilities divided by total shareholder's equity. (It is also calculated as total long-term liabilities divided by total shareholder's equity.)

This ratio reveals a company's leverage. The bigger the number, the greater the claim bond holders can place on assets. I prefer the ratio be no larger than 0.5, though capital-intensive companies may have higher ratios.

Receivables Turnover

Accounts receivable divided by sales.

A measure of how quickly company is paid by its customers. There is some fluctuation, so it is good to know the historical average. Any movement outside the range is a reason to investigate. It is not comparable across industries.

Inventory Turnover

Cost of goods sold divided by the average value of inventory.

A measure of how quickly a company goes through its inventory. The higher the number, the more quickly stockpiles turn over. You want the number to be within the historical range for the company and in line with its peers. It is not comparable across industries.

Inventory could jump near the end of a quarter because a big order was placed or is expected to be placed. This can result in a sharp rise in inventories without a corresponding change in revenues because of the timing. Management should be open about the increase and you should see inventory levels brought back into historical norms in future quarters.

If the only thing you do is look at these five ratios, you will have a good assessment of the strength or weakness of the balance sheet. Analyzing the balance sheet is better, but these ratios work well for doing a quick analysis.

KEY CHAPTER POINTS

1. The balance sheet is unique among financial metrics because it is a snapshot of one day, rather than a running account of how business is doing.
2. In general, shareholders want a company to have a lot of cash and equity.
3. The amount of cash, inventory, fixed assets, intangible assets, and debt will vary based on the industry in which company operates. It is best to compare a company's balance sheet against that of its peers and not other companies operating in different industries.
4. Five ratios that can assess the strength or weakness of a company's balance sheet: current ratio, quick ratio, debt/equity, receivables turnover, and inventory turnover.

CHAPTER 6

The Income Statement

The income statement is the most analyzed piece of financial data, and with good reason. It is the scorecard of a company's performance. With a quick glance, you can tell if a company is making or losing money. This is critical because a company's worth is often based on its profitability After all, if a corporation is not trying to maximize profits then why does it exist?

The income statement tells you more than a company's profitability. It shows if sales and earnings are increasing or decreasing and reveals if the company is making a large or small profit relative to sales. It can even tell you if the company is spending too much money on salaries, marketing, and overhead costs.

As simple as the income statement may seem, what is behind the numbers is the stuff of accounting lore. Various rules and loopholes can make for a complex system of calculating the numbers. But you do not have to be an expert in FASB (Financial Accounting Standards Board) guidelines to analyze the income statement. You have to possess a basic knowledge of what the numbers represent and the ability to analyze basic trends.

Before I explain the line items on the income statement, understand the income statement is cumulative. The income statement shows total revenues, expenses, and profits for a designated period.

For instance, when a company reports second-quarter results, the income statement shows the total revenues, expenses, and income generated for the period of April 1 through June 30. Every dollar billed, spent, or earned will be accounted for.

As stated in Chapter 6, the balance sheet is a snapshot of a single day. The balance sheet shows assets and liabilities of a company at the close of business on June 30. It tells you nothing about how the balance sheet looked on June 29. (The income statement includes both what happened on June 29 and June 30.)

The income statement gives you a running total of the business's performance, while the balance sheet focuses on a single day.

INCOME STATEMENT COMPONENTS

The Table below shows Caterpillar's (CAT) liabilities.

PERIOD ENDING	31-Dec-08	31-Dec-07	31-Dec-06
Total Revenue	51,324,000	44,958,000	41,517,000
Cost of Revenue	38,415,000	32,326,000	29,549,000
Gross Profit	12,909,000	12,332,000	11,968,000
Operating Expenses			
Research Development	1,728,000	1,404,000	1,347,000
Selling General and Administrative	4,399,000	4,875,000	4,677,000
Non Recurring	-	-	-
Others	-	-	-
Total Operating Expenses	-	-	-
Operating Income or Loss	6,782,000	6,053,000	5,944,000
Income from Continuing Operations			
Total Other Income/Expenses Net	(882,000)	320,000	214,000
Earnings Before Interest and Taxes	5,900,000	6,373,000	6,158,000
Interest Expense	1,427,000	1,420,000	1,297,000
Income Tax Expense	953,000	1,485,000	1,405,000
Minority Interest	-	-	-
Net Income From Continuing Ops	3,577,000	3,541,000	3,537,000
Non-Recurring Events			
Discontinued Operations	-	-	-
Extraordinary Items	-	-	-
Effect of Accounting Changes	-	-	-
Other Items	-	-	-
Net Income	3,557,000	3,541,000	3,537,000
Preferred Stock And Other Adjustments	-	-	-
Net Income Applicable To Common Shares	67,782,000	56,132,000	50,879,000

Handwritten margin notes: TOP LINE (pointing to Total Revenue), BOTTOM LINE (pointing to Net Income).

Revenue

Also called sales, this is the money paid to a company for the provision of goods and services. This is often referred to as the top line because it is the first item on the income statement.

Revenues can be recorded at the time a transaction is made or can be accrued over time. Companies providing services often use accrual accounting because costs are incurred over several quarters or years. By recording revenues in quarterly increments, the company provides a more accurate representation of its performance.

Sometimes companies will report net sales. This number factors in any discounts, returns or allowances provided to customers. For example, a company may give a percentage discount in exchange for faster payment. If a company does report net sales, that figure should be analyzed instead of gross sales because it reflects the true amount of transactions.

If a sale is made on credit, the transaction will be recorded on the income statement, while on the balance sheet accounts receivable will increase. However, if the buyer pays before the end of the quarter, no change will appear in accounts receivable, while revenues will still show an increase. There is a link between revenues and the balance sheet, but it is not a direct tie.

Cost of Revenue

Also commonly called cost of goods sold, this is the amount a company spends manufacturing, fabricating or producing a product.

Cost of revenue is related to inventory. Inventory is the raw materials and parts that a company acquires to produce a product. As supplies are drawn out of inventory, a deduction is made from the balance sheet and the cost of those materials is reported as an expense on the income statement. The expense is the price a company paid for those materials. This price can be determined either through FIFO (first in, first out) or LIFO (last in, first out) accounting. FIFO works best when the cost of materials is rising, because the older materials have a lower price associated with them. LIFO works best when the cost of materials is falling, because the newest materials have the lowest cost.

Though cost of revenue is dependent on the inventory's price, the inventory amount displayed on the balance sheet can and does vary from cost of revenue because a company can add or subtract from its stockpiles without impacting the income statement over the short-term.

There also may be labor or other expenses directly related to the production of products; these would also be included in cost of revenue.

Service companies may use the term "cost of services" or "cost of services provided." This is the same as cost of revenue, but providing services involves more labor than providing physical products.

Gross Profit (and Gross Margin)

Gross profit is the amount of money a company earns on all products sold or services provided within a certain period (e.g., a quarter or a year); revenue minus cost of revenue. A company not generating gross profit will have difficultly staying in business unless it can secure additional funding.

Gross margin is the percentage profit a company makes on goods sold. It is cost of revenue divided by revenues. Gross margins vary by industry and economic cycle. Specialty products that customers must have command bigger gross margins, such as medicines. Products or services not discernable by customers tend to have lower gross margins. Grocery stores are a good example—a box of Cheerios is the same product wherever you buy it so you might as well pay the lowest price.

The key for any company is maximize gross margin as much as possible. When the company is able to raise prices beyond the increase in its costs, the company is said to have pricing power. This means the vendor can demand its customers pay more for the same product. This is a good thing for shareholders because it helps increase gross margins. When a company is forced to cut prices, regardless of what is happening with inventory costs, it is said to lack pricing power. This is a bad thing for shareholders because it causes gross margins to decrease.

Selling, General & Administrative Expenses

Also known as SG&A, this is what the company spends on overhead. This broad category can include marketing, human resources, rent, utilities, office supplies, website development, legal fees, etc. Any expense that comes from normal business operations but is not directly tied to the creation of a product is accounted for here.

Consider a car. The steel, paint, leather, and plastic required to produce the car are accounted for under cost of revenue. Insurance for workers, the plant's security, the expense of keeping the plant clean, and even workmen's compensation are all overhead costs and are accounted as SG&A.[1]

Though there are rules governing what is a cost of revenue and what is a SG&A expense, companies do have some flexibility in how they assign costs. The accounting for both should be straightforward.

Research & Development (R&D)

As the name implies, the amount of money spent on researching and developing new products and services (or improving existing ones).

The amount of money spent here is debated because many R&D expenditures fail to result in a profitable product. On the other hand, constant innovation is required to grow and thwart competitive pressures. As a result, R&D expenditures should be considered as both a percentage of revenues and in the context of the company's product lines. Rising R&D expenditures are harmful if the company has a history of introducing unsuccessful products. Conversely, steady or declining R&D expenses may be positive if the company has a history of successful products. If a new, successful product is launched, the company may temporarily shift money away from R&D and into marketing. This is warranted if doing so results in higher sales.

Depreciation and Amortization

Depreciation is the decline in value for the company's fixed assets over the time covered by the income statement. Machinery, buildings, and vehicles all lose value over time from age and wear-and-tear. This decline is accounted for through depreciation expense.

Amortization is the decline in value for intangible assets. Patents, copyrights, and other intellectual property lose value as the rights near expiration. Like depreciation, this loss is accounted for on the income statement.

Depreciation and amortization are non-cash charges. The company does not spend any money because a machine's resale value is less than it was a year ago. Shareholders do realize a loss on the underlying value of the net assets. To account for this loss, a non-cash expense is deducted on the income statement.

---

[1] SG&A can be used to determine if a company is actually realizing cost savings ("synergies") from a merger. If joining forces benefits shareholders, then revenues should increase and costs should decrease as a percentage of revenues. If not, re-evaluate your decision to invest in the company.

As depreciation and amortization are deducted from the income statement, the expense is also recorded on the balance sheet. The balance sheet shows the cost paid for the fixed asset (or assigned value for the intellectual asset). Subtracted from this is the total depreciation for the asset. The difference is the income statement shows the expense for one quarter or year, whereas the balance sheet shows the fully depreciated value. Remember: the income statement shows what happened over a period of time while the balance sheet shows you the value of assets and liabilities on a specific day.

Unusual Expense (Income)

These are one-time operating expenses. It is not very common to see them and they are often grouped into other operating expenses. If they are of significant size, investigate.

Other Operating Expenses

Any expense not classified in one of the other line items is recorded here. Companies will often detail what these expenses are in their quarterly earnings release or in their SEC filings. These expenses can include, but are not limited to, legal costs and consulting fees. If these expenses are of a significant size, investigate.

Operating Income and Operating Margins

Operating income is the total amount a company makes from its regular business operations. It is gross income less SG&A, depreciation and amortization, unusual expenses, and other operating expenses.

Operating margin is operating income divided by revenues. This will always be smaller than gross margins because it factors in the cost of overhead and the decline in value for fixed assets.

Interest Income and Expense

If a company has long-term debt, it is paying bondholders interest on the loans. At the same time, the company is likely earning interest on its cash and money market balances. The difference between these amounts is displayed near the bottom of the income statement. For example, some websites display interest income as a positive number and interest expense as a negative number shown in red.

Other sites may present interest income with a minus sign or parentheses and interest expense as a positive number. The rationale for doing this is because the line items between revenues and income are considered expenses, so any amount that adds to profit should be shown as a negative number. The amount listed in this line item will be subtracted from revenues. To add an amount back in, it needs to be shown as a negative.

Other Non-Operating (Income) and Expenses

It is possible a company will generate income or expenses not directly related to its normal business operations. This could be gains or losses related to foreign exchange, commodity hedges, the sale of inventory or raw materials or other similar activity.

Outside of hedges against currency and commodity price moves, the amounts listed here should reflect one-time or infrequent transactions. If there is any amount of significant size listed here, it should be questioned.

As is the case with interest income and expense, some websites display other income as a positive number and other expenses as a negative number shown in red. Other sites may do the opposite, presenting other income as a negative number and other expenses as a positive number.

Net Income Before Taxes

Also called pre-tax income, this is revenues less all of the expenses previously described. It is the amount of income the company, in theory, pays taxes on. In reality, it might be advantageous for the company to calculate its income in one manner for the IRS and in another manner for shareholders. This can occur when there is a difference between GAAP and tax laws.

Income Taxes

The amount of money the company paid in taxes. An unusual variance in this number, particularly as a percentage of revenues, can result if there are special situations allowing the company to pay a lower tax rate or forcing it to pay a higher tax rate. Many CFOs are forthcoming about an unusual tax situation or if they expect the tax rate to change.

Minority Interest

If a company holds a majority, but not full ownership of a subsidiary, it cannot lay claim to the entire stream of profits (or losses) from the subsidiary. Rather, the amount of income (loss) attributable to the minority stakeholder must be deleted from the parent company's income statement.

For instance, say Subsidiary A earned $1 million. Parent Company owns 80% of Subsidiary A and Minority Stakeholder owns 20%. Parent Company will consolidate Subsidiary A's results into its income statement and subtract 20% of the income stream, which should be allocated to Minority Stakeholder. The largest owner has to allocate a portion of the income stream to the smaller owner.

Equity in Affiliates

Income generated from an investment in another company. Such profits are recorded here if the size of the investment is not large enough to warrant treating the secondary company as subsidiary.

Discontinued Operations

Occasionally a company will sell or shut down a division. The income or expense related to that division will be displayed at the bottom of the income statement. It is considered to be a one-time and extraordinary event because the company will no longer be financially involved with the operation.

These should be infrequent expenses unless the company is a large conglomerate with many divisions. If constant restructuring is occurring, it may be that the CEO is trying to hide bad business decisions by constantly shutting down divisions.

Net Income

The profits available to shareholders after all expenses and taxes are paid. This appears at the bottom of the income statement and is referred to as the bottom line.

Basic and Diluted Shares

Basic shares are the total amount of shares outstanding as of the date of the income statement.

Diluted shares are the total amount of shares outstanding if all options, warrants, convertible bonds, and convertible preferred shares were turned into common stock. "Diluted" means if everyone eligible to obtain common stock does, the current shareholders would see their ownership interest decrease (or diluted). In other words, the current shareholders' piece of the ownership pie would shrink.

Remember the amount of net income does not change regardless of how many shares are outstanding. What does change is how much net income is designated to each share of stock. The more shares outstanding, the lower the percentage ownership interest each share represents.

The number of diluted shares should always be used when calculating earnings per share.

QUICK ANALYSIS: THE INCOME STATEMENT

Analyzing an income statement is about looking for trends and changes in those trends. Are revenues growing? Are margins holding steady or improving? Are earnings better than a year ago?

Scale Matters

Before I start with the analysis, I want to discuss an often-overlooked point: scale matters. Every percentage point a company shows in growth means that much more additional products or services need to be provided.

For instance, Coca-Cola (KO) increased case volume during the first half of 2009 by 3%. Now 3% may not sound like much until you consider a case is 24 eight-ounce servings and during the first half of 2009, Coca-Cola sold 200 million more cases than it did during the first half of 2008. To put these numbers in perspective, Coca-Cola sold the equivalent of 3.2 billion cans of Coke more than it did the year before[2]. To do this, the beverage company had to acquire the additional ingredients (e.g., corn syrup, Aspartame), package it, and get it to bottlers. It also had to coordinate the additional supply with its bottlers to ensure excessive inventory does not accumulate in a warehouse.

Now Coca-Cola is a large corporation with many talented and experienced managers. It also has a well-developed distribution system via its bottlers. So managing growth should not be an issue. There are physical restraints as to how much Coca-Cola can grow without expanding its facilities and/or markets. (Physical restraints apply to all companies.)

For a smaller company, growth can be daunting. An increase of $100 million in revenues for company the size of Coca-Cola is manageable; a similar

---

[2] A typical can of soda holds 12 ounces.

increase for a company that only generated $125 million in sales the year before is a massive feat. Additional staff needs to be hired, additional manufacturing facilities need to be accessed, and distribution networks have to be further developed; not to mention what needs to happen with accounting, human resources, and customer service. Growth can be a difficult task to manage and many companies fail miserably. When venture capitalists invest in privately held companies they put new people in management positions; it takes a lot of business acumen to manage growth.

Also consider the size of the market. For any product, there is a limit to how much people will buy. At a certain point people do not see the need or have the desire to buy more of the same product. If a single, trendy product (or line of products) is the company's primary driver of growth, it can be problematic, as has been the case with Krispy Kreme Doughnut (KKD). The company was able to add many new locations and franchisees as its doughnuts grew in popularity. But once consumers' tastes changed, sales began to drop. Since 2005, KKD has reported declining revenues for four consecutive fiscal years.

It is critical for a company to defend its market share and constantly innovate. Some companies are good at accomplishing both, but there are many more who are not. Always consider what the numbers represent and make sure you understand the business model[3].

Revenue

At the most basic level, you want to see revenues increase. If the numbers keep getting bigger, things are going in the right direction. But to truly understand what is going on with sales, you have to look past the top line numbers and do some reading.

The time period for comparison varies by industry. In general, you want to see revenues higher now than they were for the same period the year before. However, for many industries, you also want to see sequential quarterly growth. This means revenues are higher now than they were three months ago.

On the other hand, some industries are seasonal, such as retailers, because much of their business occurs in November and December. Similarly, carmakers shut down in the summer to retool for new models. Therefore comparing a traditionally slow quarter against a traditionally busy quarter does not make sense.

Revenues also require you to conduct analysis away from the income statement. Total revenues only show what sales were, not the composition of

---

[3] Business models were discussed in Chapter 4.

those sales. In the earnings release a company will discuss the composition of revenues; this is an explanation of where sales come from. Look for signs the sales stream is sustainable and that new products are being accepted. Also keep an eye on trends for key products. If demand for key products is slipping and newer products do not comprise a substantial amount of sales, the company could be in trouble. Finally, if the company depends on subscription or some other type of recurring revenue, check to see if the trend is increasing or decreasing.

If the company discusses a new revenue recognition method or you do not understand the revenues' accounting, ask questions. There may be a legitimate reason for the accounting policy or the CFO may be trying to cover up bad business conditions. Never invest in a company if you do not understand how it makes money.

Gross Profit/Gross Margin

This can be your first sign of how the business is performing. You want to see gross profit and gross margins widening. If they are getting smaller, the company could have trouble moving its products. Gross margins are good to analyze because they directly reflect the difference between what a company charges and its cost for producing a product. As soon as a company starts to cut prices, gross margins will decline.

Lower gross margins can signify the company is encountering higher costs for its raw materials and inventory. During periods of economic growth or other favorable business conditions, suppliers can use the higher costs to push through price increases. During the commodity bubble of 2008, some companies declared "force majeure," a term that allowed them to charge above the price stipulated in a signed contract. This increased costs for the corporations who needed to buy raw materials, such as steel.

Falling gross margins are not always a bad thing. A company might find greater success with a product that is less profitable on a per-unit basis. If the lower price increases sales more than enough to offset the reduced margins, gross profits will increase. A lower price may also mean better market share and/or less competition. Generally, if a company is able to improve business by reducing gross margins, the CEO or the CFO will say so. Then it is matter of evaluating the shift and determining whether you agree with the change.

Beware if gross margins are narrow, especially if they are 10% or less. Such small gross margins suggest the company lacks pricing power (the ability to raise prices) and does not have room to absorb unanticipated costs. Such low margins occur when customers do not perceive a great value between one vendor and another.

Interest (Income) and Expense

Though it is good to see interest expense trending lower, an increase is not necessarily a negative. If a company uses debt to expand the business or purchase machinery, it can be an effective use of capital. The interest coverage ratio, which I will soon explain, can tell you if a company has a manageable level of debt.

Interest income can be an issue if it is too high. Earning some money off the cash balance is a good thing, but if it accounts for a significant proportion of pre-tax earnings, questions need to be asked. A large amount of interest income can make earnings look better than they are. Therefore, it would be beneficial to calculate pre-tax income excluding the interest income to see the company's true earnings power.

Discontinued Operations

As previously stated, discontinued operations expenses should be infrequent. If a company constantly lists discontinued operations, management could be trying to hide that the business is not well-operated.

Net Income and Earnings per Share

It is not uncommon for investors to look at earnings per share to determine if earnings are growing. The problem is EPS can be manipulated through stock repurchase programs. As a company buys back stock, the amount of earnings attributable to each share rises. Therefore, stock repurchase programs can make it appear a company grew earnings when it has not. The more prudent analysis would be to ensure both net income and earnings per share are growing.

Net Margin

Net margin is net income divided by total revenues; it calculates the company's profitability. If net margins are small, 5% or less, the company may have little flexibility to cut costs should business conditions worsen. On the other hand, if net margins are too big, competitors will look for a way to take away business.

Ideally, net margins should be steady or increasing and slightly better than the industry average.

Return on Equity (ROE)
Net income divided by shareholder equity[4].

ROE, one of the most commonly used ratios, is a measure of management effectiveness; it calculates the return management generates from the shareholders' stake in the company. ROE varies by industry, so it is important to compare a company against its peers instead of a company in a different sector. Preferably you want to invest in a company with a higher ROE than its peers.

RATIOS AND STATISTICS
In addition to ROE, there are various ratios and statistics used to measure how well a company performs. Here are the some of the most common ratios used in conjunction with the income statement.

Return on Assets (ROA)
Net income divided by total assets.

This calculates how effectively management uses the firm's assets to generate income. The difference between ROE and ROA: ROA does not factor in the company's financial structure. A firm with a significant level of debt can have a high ROE (due to a small amount of shareholder equity) and a low ROA (due to a large amount of assets). For most investors, looking at ROE is sufficient.

Interest Coverage Ratio
Earnings before interest and taxes (EBIT) divided by interest expense.

This ratio calculates a company's ability to make its interest payments. Ratios of 1.0 mean the company's earnings cover interest payments and nothing else. This ratio can be included in debt agreements. Should the ratio fall below a certain level, bond holders can force a liquidation of the assets.

EBITDA
Some companies like to use EBITDA (pronounced "Eee-Bit-Dah") instead of actual earnings. EBITDA stands for "earnings before interest, taxes, depreciation, and amortization." EBITDA is used when the company has a large amount of

---

[4] Shareholder equity is located on the balance sheet. See Chapter 5.

debt and high deprecation costs. Some CEOs claim that EBITDA provides a more accurate representation of how the business performs.

I have never been a big fan of EBITDA because a company is either making money or it is not. However, if EBITDA is used in the industry to assess corporate performance, the cash flow statement needs to be scrutinized. I will you show how to do this in the next chapter.

Funds From Operations (FFO)

Net income plus depreciation and amortization.

FFO, used by REITs, is a measure of how much cash flow the partnership is generating. Because depreciation expense from owning land and buildings is so high, net income does not provide a proper measure of how the partnership is really performing.

Book-to-Bill

The number of orders received (booked) divided by the number of products shipped (billed).

Book-to-bill is a measure of future revenue streams. The higher the number, the more likely revenues will increase. Keep in mind that orders can be canceled, so the book-to-bill ratio will not always be an accurate forecasting tool.

Backlog

The amount of unfilled orders.

This is a dollar amount provided by some companies. Like book-to-bill, it is not always an accurate forecasting tool because orders can be canceled.

Load Factor

How much a plane's capacity is used by paying customers or cargo.

Higher numbers are better because it means more of the plane's capacity is being used. Even one empty seat or small amount of unfilled cargo area is a revenue opportunity lost.

Same-Store Sales (comparable store-sales or comp store-sales)

The change in revenues for locations open for a year or more.

This is a more accurate measure of growth for the retail industry because it shows if existing locations are seeing growth or contraction. Low- to mid-single digit percentage growth is good. Low double-digit growth or higher is great, but not sustainable. Contraction, obviously, is bad.

KEY CHAPTER POINTS

1. The income statement is cumulative; it gives you a running total of how the business is performing, while the balance sheet focuses on a single day.

2. Scale matters because the higher the rate of growth, the more difficult it is to manage.

3. Revenues and earnings should grow over time. Ideally gross and net margins should also improve over time. A trend of narrowing margins should be a warning sign, unless the company has proven it can offset the lower margins through higher sales.

4. If interest income accounts for a significant proportion of pre-tax earnings, it could be making earnings look better than they really are. In such cases, calculate pre-tax income excluding income to determine how the business is performing.

5. Check to see if net income is actually increasing, as earnings per share growth can be inflated by stock buyback programs.

6. ROE varies by industry; compare a company against its peers instead of a company in a different sector.

CHAPTER 7

The Cash Flow Statement

Of the three financial statements, the cash flow statement is my favorite. Glance at a few key items and you can tell if profits are rising, normal business operations are generating (or burning through) cash, dividends are paid and the company is increasing or paying down debt. Furthermore, the cash flow statement is less likely to be influenced by accounting practices than the income statement.

The cash flow statement is unique because it ties the balance sheet and the income statement together. It indicates if a company's cash balance has increased or decreased and serves as a running scorecard of how much money is coming into and going out. The cash flow statement calculates if the company is generating more cash than it spends. It also tells you what sources are supplying cash and how the company is spending its cash.

Realize there is a difference between earnings and cash. Earnings are an accounting figure. A company can earn $10 million by selling products and services. However, if it is spending $15 million on new equipment, additional inventories, debt repayment, and stock buyback programs, its cash balance will decline by $5 million. Anyone with a credit card or access to a line of credit knows his ability to spend is not tied to his level of income. As a shareholder you want the company to show that, over time, it is generating more cash thn it spends. If this does not occur, the company will be forced to take on additional debt or sell more stock—both could have negative implications.

CASH FLOW STATEMENT COMPONENTS

The cash flow statement is broken into three sections: Cash from Operating Activities, Cash from Investing, and Cash from Financing Activities. Each refers to a method used to raise or spend cash. Their totals are combined to determine if net cash is increasing or decreasing.

The Table below shows Caterpillar's (CAT) cash flows.

PERIOD ENDING	31-Dec-08	31-Dec-07	31-Dec-06
Net Income	3,557,000	3,541,000	3,537,000
Operating Activities, Cash Flows Provided By or Used In			
Depreciation	1,980,000	1,797,000	1,602,000
Adjustments to Net Income	383,000	199,000	197,000
Changes In Accounts Receivables	(545,000)	899,000	(89,000)
Changes In Liabilities	715,000	2,178,000	1,614,000
Changes In Inventory	(833,000)	(745,000)	(827,000)
Changes In Other Operating Activities	(470,000)	66,000	(235,000)
Total Cash Flow From Operating Activities	4,787,000	7.935.000	5,799,000
Investing Activities, Cash Flows Provided By or Used In			
Captial Expenditures	(4,011,000)	(3,040,000)	(2,675,000)
Investments	(3,464,000)	(2,237,000)	(2,016,000)
Other Cashflows from Investing Activities	1,179,000	869,000	895,000
Total Cash Flows From Investing Activities	(6,296,000)	(4,408,000)	(3,796,000)
Financing Activities, Cash Flows Provided By or Used In			
Dividends Paid	(953,000)	(845,000)	(726,000)
Sale Purchase of Stock	(1,703,000)	(2,133,000)	(2,794,000)
Net Borrowings	5,565,000	(146,000)	758,000
Other Cash Flows from Financing Activities	56,000	155,000	169,000
Total Cash Flows From Financing Activities	2,965,000	(2,969,000)	(2,593,000)
Effect of Exchange Rate Changes	158,000	34,000	12,000
Change In Cash and Cash Equivalents	$1,614,000	$592,000	($578,000)

CASH FROM OPERATING ACTIVITIES

Also referred to as "cash from operations," this component shows whether normal business operations are generating or consuming cash. A positive number means the company is bringing in more cash than it spends ("cash-flow positive"). A negative number means the company is spending more cash than it is bringing in ("cash-flow negative"). A company spending more than it brings in can be described as "burning through cash."

Cash from operating activities is important because a company can only spend more than it brings in for a limited time before looking for outside financing. A rapidly growing company will have negative cash flow, but cash from operating activities needs to turn positive for the company to survive.

On the other hand, a company that is contracting can be cash-flow positive for a period of time. This occurs because the company has to spend less to maintain its business. For example, fewer sales mean less need to buy additional raw materials for inventory. Eventually, the company will either go bankrupt or shrink to a size where it can survive, but with considerably lower profits and cash flow.

Cash from operating activities is calculated from net income, depreciation (and depletion), amortization, deferred taxes, non-cash items, and changes in working capital.

Net Income

The profits available to shareholders after all expenses and taxes are paid. This line item is pulled from the income statement.

Depreciation (and Depletion)

Depreciation is a non-cash expense, meaning it does not require spending any cash. It is an accounting figure that measures the decrease in a fixed asset's value (e.g., the decline in the value of your new car that occurs the minute you drive it off the lot). Depreciation lowers net income but has no impact on the company's cash balance, so it is added back on the cash flow statement. Depreciation is pulled from the income statement.

Depletion may also be listed here, if the company has interests in natural resources. Depletion refers to the carrying cost of those assets and includes the resulting devaluation as the resources are removed. An example would be the reduction in oil reserves as crude is taken out of the ground. Like depreciation, depletion reduces the amount of assets on the balance sheet and is a non-cash expense on the income statement.

Amortization

Like depreciation, amortization is a non-cash expense. It is an accounting figure that measures the decline in value of a non-tangible asset, such as a patent. (As patents move closer to expiration, they decline in value.) Amortization lowers net income, but it does not require any outlay of cash. Therefore, it is added back to the cash flow statement.

To better explain the math, consider the difference between the income statement and the cash flow statement. An asset's loss of value reduces shareholder equity, or "costs" shareholders. These costs are accounted for by reducing net income. However, they do not require the outlay of any money. For example, the decline in your car's value has no impact on your checking account balance, even though the decline lowers your net worth. The cash flow statement starts off with net income and adjusts it by adding back any non-cash expenses.

Depreciation and amortization are treated as expenses on the income statement because they lower shareholder equity. This accounting treatment reduces net income, so both amounts need to be added back to the cash flow statement to accurately show how much cash the company actually generated (or used).

Deferred Taxes

Since tax laws can vary from GAAP, it may be advantageous for a company to pay a big tax bill up front and deduct the expense from earnings over the next several years. This often occurs when a company uses one method of depreciation for taxes and another for reporting to shareholders.

As the tax expense is realized on the income statement, earnings are reduced. But because the company spent the money to pay for the tax liability, no cash for the current period was used. Therefore, deferred taxes are a non-cash expense and increase the amount of cash from operating activities.

Non-Cash Items

A company may also recognize other non-cash expenses on its income statement, including prepaid expenses or other accrued expenses, such as the one-time cost for rearranging facilities. (The expense would be recognized over time because the improved production yields a long-term benefit.) The recognition of these expenses does not have any impact on cash for the current period, therefore they are added back to increase actual cash flows.

Changes in Working Capital

This line item can either be summarized or broken into more detail, depending on the presentation of the cash flow statement. A summary indicates how current net assets have increased or decreased. Cash spent on acquiring inventory and paying bills reduces the company's cash flow. Conversely, bills that are due, but not paid, increase the cash balance.

This is one area where the balance sheet impacts the cash flow statement. A company experiencing strong growth will see its cash balance reduced as it spends significantly on raw materials and other items to increase inventories. This is a cash outlay. Invoices sent to customers that have not been paid also reduce the cash balance. (The company spent money on providing the products but has not been paid for those products by the customer.) On the other hand, a company can increase its cash balance by being slow to pay its own bills. The money might be owed, but until the bill is paid, the firm's cash balance is inflated.

Total Cash from Operating Activities

This is the sum of all the previous line items. Non-cash and prepaid expenses are added to net income, while increases in inventory or other paid expenses incurred as part of normal business operations are deducted. You want positive numbers here.

CASH FROM INVESTING ACTIVITIES

In addition to spending cash on normal business operations, a company needs to spend money on fixed assets, such as machinery or a new building. As such expenditures are long-term in nature, they are recorded as investments. The rationale behind separating operating expenditures (e.g., raw materials), and fixed assets (e.g., furniture) is to show how much cash the company generates from normal business operations and how much it spends on items appearing on the balance sheet for more than 12 months.

Investments in other companies and other long-term expenditures are also listed here.

Capital Expenditures

How much money is spent on fixed assets such as machinery, vehicles, buildings, furniture, fixtures, etc. The amounts can vary from year to year, depending on the timing of the purchases. If there is a big increase, the company may document the purchase in its quarterly report or discuss it during the quarterly earnings conference call. A call to the investor relations department should be able to clarify the expenditure.

This line item also includes cash received from the sale of a fixed asset. Though most often displayed as a negative number (cash spent on new fixed assets), capital expenditures can be positive if the company sells more assets (cash in from sellers) than it buys (cash out to vendors).

Other Investing Activities

Any long-term expenditure not previously categorized that is not part of normal business operations. Examples include the acquisition or disposition of a subsidiary and purchase or sale of an investment, such as a joint venture or commodity and currency hedges.

Total Cash from Investing Activities

The total amount of cash spent or received from investing activities. Often this will be a negative number because companies are reinvesting their profits so the business will grow.

CASH FROM FINANCING ACTIVITIES

A business can receive funds from four main sources: profits (cash from operating activities), the sale of assets and business units (cash from investing), offering stock, and borrowing money. The latter two are financing activities because the company is either selling part of itself (via a stock offering) or borrowing from lenders. Any money received from or paid to shareholders or bond holders is shown as cash from financing.

Financing Cash Flow Items

A transaction other than the payment of dividends, purchase/offering of stock or payment/issuance of debt related to the company's capital structure.

Dividends

Dividends are a financing activity because they represent the distribution of profits to shareholders. They are listed as a negative because they represent cash paid out.

Issuance (Retirement) of Stock

Offerings of stock, whether an initial public offering (IPO) or secondary offering, raise cash for the company. Share repurchase (buyback) programs require cash to be spent. In both cases, these sums represent money received from or paid to shareholders.

The key difference between this and the sale of an investment is that the company is altering its ownership structure. Shareholders are either seeing their ownership diluted (issuance of new shares) or increased (repurchase of stock). Conversely, the sale of an investment or a business unit may have no impact on the company's ownership structure.

Issuance (Retirement) of Debt

When a long-term term loan is secured or a bond offering completed, the company receives an inflow of cash. Though liabilities are increased on the balance sheet, the new debt increases the amount of cash available to be spent.

The repayment of debt reduces cash flow. The company diverts money it would otherwise have to pay down its debt. Though the repayment of debt is a positive, it is displayed as a negative on the cash flow statement. (Consider your car payment: by making payments, you decrease the amount of money you owe. At the same time, you decrease your checking account balance, lowering the amount of money you have to save or spend.)

Total Cash from Financing Activities

The total inflows or outflows from financing activities. Though this total is helpful to gauge the overall impact on cash flows, it is important to look at the previous line items and determine how the company raises or distributes cash.

FOREIGN EXCHANGE EFFECTS

This is an accounting entry designed to reconcile differences caused by the translation of cash flows generated in different currencies.

An example would be a company with operations in the United States, Europe, Japan, and China. This company would generate cash in U.S. dollars, euros, yen, and yuan. Though there are rules designed to handle how currency is translated, accounting rules allow for a special line item to ensure the cash flow statement accurately shows the money flowing between the income statement and the balance sheet.

A reconciliation, *Effect of Exchange Rate Changes*, is a separate line item on the cash flow statement, separate from the other three components.

NET CHANGE IN CASH

How much of a company's cash balance increased or decreased. It is the sum of Cash from Operating Activities, Cash from Investing Activities, Cash from Financing Activities, and the Effect of Exchange Rate Changes. Positive numbers mean the company has more cash now than it did at the start of the period. Negative numbers mean the company has less cash.

QUICK ANALYSIS: CASH FLOW STATEMENT

Logic would seem to dictate all a person need do is scroll to the bottom of the cash flow statement and see if the net change is positive or negative. After all, if a company is profitable and run correctly, it should be generating cash, right? Unfortunately, it is not so simple.

The reasons a company's cash balance has changed are just as important as the change itself. The cash balance can be increased every year by taking out new debt, offering new stock or not investing money back into the business. Though none of this benefits shareholders over the long-term, it does generate cash. Therefore, it is important to look through the cash flow statement to determine how money is brought in and where it is spent.

When I review a cash flow statement, I look at if the business model is making money and the company is acting in the best interest of its shareholders. Even a cursory review can give me enough information to know if the company deserves more research.

Net Income

Though net income is also listed on the income statement, it can be convenient to look at it on the cash flow statement first—particularly because it appears at the top. (In comparison, net income appears near the bottom of the income statement.)

The company should be profitable and have a history of growth (barring any periods of economic distress as the country experienced in 2009). There should also be some consistency with the trend—a year that shows a large increase or decrease is cause for further examination. There could have been an unusual event, such as an acquisition or a divesture, or a problem with the business. The income statement will shed more light on what happened.

Cash Flow from Operating Activities

I want to know if the business model is generating cash. I want to see positive numbers for most years, and preferably growth over time. If the business model works and the company is well managed, it should have positive cash flow. A firm with negative cash flow year after year will either need to raise more debt or sell additional stock to fund normal operations—not a good thing.

Payment of Dividends

A regular dividend policy can force the CEO and CFO to make more prudent fiscal decisions because dividend payments require the allocation of cash. Conversely, a stock buyback program does not have to be completed. A company can choose to repurchase fewer shares than shareholders expect without experiencing the negative stigma a missed dividend payment would have.

If a company does pay dividends, the amount should increase over time. Such increases demonstrate a willingness by executives to maintain or increase earnings paid to the shareholders. A decrease or elimination of a dividend usually signals a problem; it may be a temporary business slump or a sign of bigger problems.

A company undergoing strong growth may not pay dividends. If the best use of capital is to fund expansion, shareholders will benefit more if no dividends are paid. Therefore, the lack of a dividend is not a bad thing, but in exchange, there should be strong growth.

Issuance of Debt

Does the company raise debt on a regular basis or is it paying back the loans? There is nothing wrong with taking out new debt if the money is used for expansion, but the company should not have to rely constantly on lenders. If more debt is raised every year, be cautious if net income does not increase at a proportionate rate.

Issuance (Repurchase of Capital Stock)

A positive number means the company is selling more stock to raise capital. Such actions are dilutive to current shareholders because they lower the amount of income attributable to each shareholder. Positive numbers indicate further investigation is necessary. Find out why the company has to go back to the equity markets.

Net Change in Cash Equivalents

This is a quick check to see if the company generates or burns through cash. This indicator alerts you that something has been overlooked on the cash flow statement, especially if negative numbers appear for most years.

ANALYSIS OF OTHER LINE ITEMS

The key for the rest of the cash flow statement is to look for unusual increases or decreases in the line items. If a significant change exists, investigate.

Depreciation

An increase in depreciation generally means the company acquired a new fixed asset. There should be an increase in cash spent on fixed assets, reflecting the purchase. (An increase in debt would not be surprising because it may make more sense to finance the purchase than pay cash.) If there is no increase in cash spent on fixed assets, the company wrote down the value of certain assets. This could reflect an adjustment for obsolete machinery or a change in business operations (e.g., the closing on a particular office).

Amortization

A large increase may reflect acquisition of a business or devaluing of intangible assets. If too high a price was paid for an acquisition, a significant charge might be taken—this can happen through the restatement of past earnings and cash flows.

Deferred Taxes and Non-Cash Items

For both line items, be wary of a significant year-over-year change. Though such a shift can occur as part of normal business operations, it may also reflect a shift in accounting policy.

Changes in Working Capital

Working capital can be volatile from the timing of orders and purchase of inventories. Nonetheless, a sharp increase or decrease in working capital should be examined. It could be an early sign the company is experiencing problems.

Capital Expenditures

Spending on capital expenditures should be in line with revenues. If revenues are not growing, but significant money is spent on property and equipment, executives may not be making smart business decisions. Alternatively, executives may be investing in a new facility or equipment to take advantage of a new business opportunity or a change in technology.

Other Investing Cash Flows

A large outflow may be cause for investigation. There could be good reasons, but if you have concerns, investigate.

Keep an eye on any big changes. You want to see a trend of increasing profits, positive cash from operating activities, and steady or increasing dividend payments. Finally, understand what is behind the change in cash. A growing company will use more cash than it generates if it is constantly investing in the business—but profits should also rise.

Pay attention to cash from operating activities; if that number is always negative, look for another stock to invest in.

KEY CHAPTER POINTS

1. The cash flow statement is unique because it ties the balance sheet and the income statement together.
2. There is a difference between earnings and cash. Earnings are an accounting figure but the cash balance relies on how much money a company spends and how much it brings in.

3. The reasons a company's cash balance has changed are just as important as the change itself.
4. If the business model works and the company is well managed, cash flows from operating activities should be positive for most years.
5. If a company pays dividends, the amount should increase over time. A decrease or elimination of a dividend usually signals a problem.
6. Be cautious if the level of debt rises every year and if net income does not increase at a proportionate rate because the company is not taking too much additional debt.
7. Always keep an eye on unusual increases or decreases in line items.

PART 3

Valuation:

Determine How Much a Stock is Worth—The Most Important Factor in Making Profitable Decisions

CHAPTER 8

The Two Most Profitable Measures of Valuation

How much is a share of stock worth?

This is not a simple question. The wrong answer can result in a substantial loss of money. Conversely, getting it right can lead to an increase in wealth. Fortunately valuation is not an exact science. Buy within the margin of error and profits should come. Ignore what the valuation measures state and not only may profits never be realized, but the risks of substantial losses are suddenly elevated.

So how much is a share of stock worth?

According to the Efficient Market Hypothesis (EMH), stocks are always priced at fair value. Fair value is the price at which a seller and a buyer, both of whom are not under pressure to engage in the transaction, would exchange assets.

As you may remember from Chapter 2, EMH states that at any time, all known information is priced into a stock. Furthermore, market participants act in a rational manner and always seek to maximize their profit opportunities. Therefore, the current selling price of a stock has to be the correct price because all known information is reflected in the price and no rational investor would pay more. Changes in price could only occur through the introduction of new information.

Short-term manias, such as the tech bubble of the late 1990s, call into question the applicability of the Efficient Market Hypothesis. Several stocks traded at valuations that did not reflect their underlying tangible value or the profits they would generate over the next several years. The defense of EMH is investors thought the future would be brighter than the current fundamentals showed (all known information is priced in) and these investors were buying tech stocks because the potential returns were so high (maximize profit opportunities). Furthermore, these investors thought projected growth rates would only be revised upward (pricing in new information).

Although these investors were trying to act in a manner that would maximize profits, there is a strong argument they were not acting rationally. Stocks were trading at P/E multiples of 200 or higher, even though their forecast growth rates were considerably lower. Even after accounting for upward revisions, valuations had reached a level where the law of numbers dictated that growth would slow[1].

The other argument was that valuations did not reflect the underlying book value of the businesses. As you will recall from Chapter 5, book value is the difference between assets and liabilities; the portion of the company actually owned by shareholders. Even with including patents, branding,[2] and other intangibles listed on the balance sheet, many tech and dot-com companies were valued at prices considerably higher than their underlying book value. Such prices implied a "going concern" value, suggesting the company was so effective at using their assets that it would generate cash for years to come. In reality, many of these companies had to curtail their operations significantly in 2001 and 2002 to stay afloat.

The corresponding drop in share prices following the tech bubble's burst suggests the markets are efficient over the long-term. Decisions to buy and sell are often made over the short-term though, and understanding if the markets are correctly pricing a stock at a given time is key to making money. To answer the question of what a share of stock is worth, I will discuss three primary

---

[1] The law of numbers says that as an amount doubles in size, it takes an exponentially larger amount to double again. For instance, it may not be that difficult for a company to increase profits from $10 million to $20 million. But for a company to double profits of $10 billion to $20 billion, it must figure out how to generate an additional $10 billion in earnings. To put this number in scale, less than 400 companies were worth more than $10 billion and only 21 companies had annual earnings in excess of $10 billion in 2009.

[2] During the tech bubble, it was possible for a company to increase the value of its branding by simply adding ".com". Euphoric valuations were assigned to many business and brand names containing the suffix, despite the fact that having a website in no way guaranteed any new revenues, much less profits.

measures of valuation in this and the next chapter: price-to-book value, price-to-earnings, and discounted cash flow. The first two will provide good measures of valuation; the third provides a sanity check to ensure you are not overpaying for a stock.

PRICE-TO-BOOK VALUE

Book value is the theoretical value of what a company's net assets are worth. It is also referred to as equity. In theory, book value is equivalent to the amount of cash shareholders would receive if all of the company's debts, both short-term and long-term, were paid off and all remaining assets were sold. Book value is the underlying value of the company.

Multiple studies have shown that price-to-book (P/B) value is the most effective valuation measure in determining a stock's performance. Although price-to-earnings (P/E) is a considerably more popular measure, buying at low P/B multiples leads to better returns.

Book value's compelling use as a measure of valuation can be explained in one statement: *No quality company should sell for a price equivalent to or less than its theoretical liquidation value.*

Applying this statement will do more to help you make money than just about any other investment concept. Benjamin Graham encouraged investors to look for companies trading near or below their book values in his 1934 book, *Securities Analysis.* Warren Buffett is believed to adhere to this concept more than 75 years later. Fortunes have been built following this statement. If you don't remember anything else from this book, remember the importance of book value.

The reason book value is such a powerful measure of valuation lies deep in the concept of what book value is and what it means to an ongoing business concern. Book value is what a company's net assets are worth. A P/B multiple of 1.0 means the company is worth the same as its net assets. This multiple means the market is indifferent as to whether the company opens its doors tomorrow. If the business is shut down, the debts paid off, and the assets liquidated, shareholders' wealth will, theoretically, be unchanged. If the company stays open, shareholders' wealth may increase or decrease. Not liquidating the company becomes a roll of the dice.

Such a view is callous. Workers depend on the company staying open to collect their salaries. Suppliers will lose business if the company closes and customers will be forced to find another vendor, and potentially pay higher prices, get a lower quality product or both. The market, though, is apathetic to whether a business opens it doors tomorrow.

Stocks are bought and sold for one reason—to make money. If the same amount of money can be made by liquidating the company as can be made by keeping the doors open, where is the incentive to believe the stock will be worth more tomorrow or the day after tomorrow? The market is telling shareholders the reward for keeping the company open is minimal.

In theory, shareholders should vote to liquidate any company below book value. In reality, a company may be worth more as a going concern than the value of its net assets. An existing company has an organizational structure encompassing management, employees, accounting procedures, customers, and suppliers. It has office equipment and may also have machinery, tools, and warehouse equipment. Intangible assets such as a brand name, a website, a physical address and phone numbers are established. Nearly all companies have marketing strategies in place, whether these strategies are simply branding or a comprehensive advertising and public relations campaign.

While this may seem immaterial to a company's worth, these intangibles are the essence of an ongoing corporation and therefore add value. For instance, suppose an extremely wealthy investor wanted to enter the soda business. He could buy an existing soda company or start his own company. If he chose the latter, he would have to acquire office space, set up bottling facilities, and establish a distribution system. In addition, he would have to hire employees, create a management structure, build a customer base, and promote his company.

Creating a business from scratch takes a lot of work and money. Even after much effort and capital is put into the venture, most companies fail within their first years of operation. The money invested in a failed corporation is not the only loss; there is also the opportunity cost of not investing the money elsewhere. Opportunity costs compound monetary losses.

The opportunity cost of investing in an ongoing concern can be lower, particularly if a good management team is in place. An existing company has a physical structure (office space, furniture, copiers, etc.), an organizational structure (a chain of management, employees, etc.) and intangibles (branding, a recognizable address, etc.). It also has procedures for acquiring necessary supplies and lines of credit. Most importantly, an established company has paying customers, distribution systems, and a method for bringing products to market. Everything necessary for a company to function is already established and operational.

A mathematical argument can be made for why an ongoing concern should not sell for near or below book value. A profitable, well-managed company will generate a return on its assets. This profit can either be maintained as cash (increasing book value), invested in new projects (potentially creating a higher stream of earnings in the future) or given back to the shareholders (dividends or stock buybacks). In any of these scenarios, shareholders may benefit more by keeping the doors open than they would by liquidating.

This can be demonstrated by using the return on equity (ROE) ratio. As stated in Chapter 6, ROE is proportionate profit generated from the company's net assets. ROE is calculated as "Net Income/Equity."

To present the mathematical argument against liquidation, let's use a fictional company with a market capitalization of $900 million and $1 billion in shareholder equity. Shares of this company trade at a P/B multiple of 0.9 ($900 million/$1 billion). During the past five years, the company has generated an average ROE of 10%. For the sake of simplicity, we will also assume that net income has increased proportionately to the increase in shareholder's equity.

If shareholders voted to liquidate the company, they stand to gain 11% on their investment. This would be a one-time gain of $100 million spread among all shareholders, whose total investment, according to the market value of the company, is $900 million.

A guaranteed return of 11% is good, but if shareholders decide to roll the dice and assume the company will continue to be profitable and generate 10% ROE in the foreseeable future, the potential gains are even bigger. In fact, in about two years, shareholders can get nearly double the return even if the stock continues to trade at a P/B multiple of 0.9.

Starting Shareholder's Equity	$1,000,000,000
Profits Retained (ROE of 10%)	+
	$100,000,000
Equity at End of Year 1	$1,100,000,000
Equity at end of Year 1	$1,100,000,000
Profits Retained (ROE of 10%)	+ $110,000,000
Equity at End of Year 2	$1,210,000,000

STARTING MARKET CAPITALIZATION

Shareholder's Equity	$1,000,000,000
P/B Multiple	x 0.9
Market Capitalization	$900,000,000

ENDING MARKET CAPITALIZATION

Shareholder's Equity	$1,210,000,000
P/B Multiple	x 0.9
Market Capitalization	$1,089,000,000

REALIZED RETURN

Ending Market Capitalization	$1,089,000,000
Starting Market Capitalization	– $900,000,000
Gain	$189,000,00
Starting Market Capitalization	/ $900,000,000
Return	21%

If a modest increase in the rate of growth is assumed, the numbers turn even more in favor of maintaining the company. For instance, assume the same company is able to generate a 5% growth rate above the increase in its net assets over the next 12 months. We know that without any growth, the company would earn $100 million (ROE of 10% x shareholder's equity of $1 billion). Factoring in the low amount of growth increases profits up to $105 million. If all the earnings are retained, shareholder's equity at the end of 12 months increases to $1.105 billion – a gain of 10.5% The table below shows the math.

A 10.5% gain may not sound spectacular, but if the company continues to maintain this modest improvement in the rate of its growth, the numbers begin to compound very quickly. After just two years, the total return jumps to 27%, versus 21% without the increase in the growth rate. If all earnings are retained, shareholder's equity jumps to $1.58 billion in five years. This equates to a nearly 60% increase.[3]

I used very simplistic models to calculate the returns for both liquidating the company and maintaining it as a going concern. Therefore, while the numbers

---

[3] To get the 60% increase, the company was assumed to have retained all profits. In reality, as a company grows, it will spend money. Therefore, the actual growth in book value would differ widely from the calculations, and so would the actual return. Nonetheless, if the company is well managed, the growth should lead to an increase in both shareholder's equity and the stock price.

do show a mathematical argument against liquidation, there are a few factors that should be taken into consideration.

Liquidation, as I will soon explain, is not a simple process. The actual proceeds realized from the liquidation are often different from the numbers stated on the balance sheet. It is nearly impossible one for an individual investor to initiate liquidation. In addition, there is the risk that any subsequent investment could

Starting Shareholder's Equity	$1,000,000,000
Return on Equity (Year 1)	x 10%
Profits	$100,000,000
Additional Profits from Growth	+ $5,000,000
Total Retained Profits	$105,000,000
Starting Shareholder's Equity	+ $1,000,000,000
Ending Shareholder's Equity	$105,000,000
Total Gain	
Total Retained Profits	$105,000,000
Starting Shareholder's Equity	+ $1,000,000,000
Gain in Shareholder's Equity	10.5%

produce a lower return than would be realized if the company were maintained as a going concern. (To be fair, it is possible that the subsequent investment could generate a higher return.)

As far as keeping the company as a going concern, we do not know for sure that management will increase shareholder's equity in the years to come. Five years from now, the actual return realized by shareholders will probably be far different than the proposed 60% gain. The company could lose money, thereby lowering the amount of retained earnings. Management could make bad decisions on how to utilize the assets. The company could go bankrupt.

On the other hand, growth could be considerably stronger than expected. Management could choose to pay dividends to shareholders. The company could be acquired at a sizable premium. The market could realize the valuation is too low and bid the price of the shares up. It is impossible to say what the future holds.

In addition, we do not know how much the company will spend on new equipment, facility expansion or marketing campaigns. Anything affecting the company's growth (e.g., the introduction of a blockbuster product) will affect the percentage of earnings retained from year to year. Because it is not possible to predict with accuracy how much a company will spend from year to year, forecasting future book value is a waste of time. Even when multiple scenarios are examined, the projected book value will be materially different from what the company actually reports.

The great thing about the P/B multiple is it does not need to be used as a forecasting tool. Rather, P/B should be used to determine one simple thing: is the market adequately recognizing a company's worth as an ongoing concern? A well-managed company trading at or near book value is too cheaply valued and therefore should be considered as a potential investment. (A rule of thumb for purchase is a P/B of 2 or lower, though 1.25 or lower is even better). A well-managed company trading at a significant premium to book value (P/B of greater than 4) should be watched, but is only suitable for speculative trading until the valuation becomes reasonable. A company that is not well-managed should never be purchased for any reason.

It is important to realize there is no magic number where a stock suddenly becomes attractive. If a company has superb management, a great business model and fiscal strength but trades at a book value of 2.25, it still should be considered for purchase. Is it a better value at a P/B of 1.25? Absolutely, but if the company is that well-managed, then it should be trading at a premium valuation anyway. It is always better to pay slightly more for a great company than slightly less for a subpar company. Never pay a high premium for a stock, but do not pass on a great quality company just because its valuation is slightly above what you would like to pay.

Put another way, what matters is if the purchase price represents a reasonable discount. If management is capable of creating shareholder value and the current price does not reflect this fact, the stock is a good value. If management is suspect and the current price reflects too much optimism about the company's prospects, the stock is overvalued. The best way to determine if a stock is undervalued relative to its prospects is book value. Great companies are always worth considerably more than the underlying value of their assets. Similarly, poorly managed companies and those with bad business models deserve to trade at valuations equivalent to the value of their assets because of their uncertain future.

THE OTHER SIDE OF BOOK VALUE – LIQUIDATION

Suppose a company is poorly managed and is trading below book value: Does it have appeal because the price is so low? There are two ways to look at this situation.

The first is to assume the company does have worth as an ongoing concern and simply needs new management. Effecting a change of management is difficult, especially because it requires a majority (or a super-majority) vote by shareholders. Furthermore, if the board members fail to recognize that current management has failed, how likely they are to find a highly competent CEO?

A competitor could acquire the company, but waiting for an acquisition to occur is a fool's game. Without controlling a majority of shares, individual shareholders cannot push management to seek a buyer. Furthermore, a potential buyer may not want to pay a premium over the current price. Even after an acquisition has been announced, there is no guarantee the merger will take place. It is not unheard of for a potential merger to be canceled.

The second alternative is liquidation: sell all the assets, pay off all of the debts, and give the remaining money to the shareholders. In theory this should generate a positive return.

If this concept were to hold true, the smartest investment strategy would be to buy poorly managed companies trading below book value and liquidate them. Returns would be nearly guaranteed. Calculating profit would boil down to simple arithmetic: Book value less market capitalization equals profit. It would make no sense to invest in a company worth more than its book value.

Unfortunately, life and investing are never that easy. If making money came down to buying poorly managed companies trading below book value and liquidating them, everyone would be doing it. The unintended effect, though, would be that valuations are pushed closer and closer to book value, thus limiting profit.[4] More dollars chasing after the same stock will boost the price. Blame it on the law of supply and demand.

Another obstacle is corporate charters. Approval by the majority or even a super-majority of shareholders is required for liquidation. Clearing this hurdle means seeking the consent of large shareholders and many small shareholders. There would also be potential lawsuits filed by dissident shareholders, objections from unions and bond holders and other hurdles created by corporate executives. Depending on the level and intensity of the objections, achieving approval for liquidation could be a lengthy and costly process.

---

[4] This would be a classic case of the Efficient Market Hypothesis in action. Rational investors, seeing the opportunity for profit, would all follow the same strategy until the ability to make money is eliminated.

There is also the problem that the amount of cash generated by the sale of a company's assets and the payment of all debts can differ from the recorded book value. Under a liquidation scenario, buyers would pay as little as possible for the assets. New payables would arise, such as accounting fees. Penalties for breaking leases and contracts could be assessed. Legal costs would present themselves, including the possibility of lawsuits by dissident shareholder groups.[5]

The asset side is just as messy. As discussed in Chapter 5, the recorded value of assets is often disconnected from the price a buyer would pay. For instance, office furniture may be fully depreciated, but still have value (e.g., there are always buyers for filing cabinets in decent condition). Inventory could be worthless, especially specialized parts, or could sell for less than its purchase price. Certain customers, knowing the company is being liquidated, may avoid paying invoices, thus making receivables worth less. Intangible items might command a dollar value unrelated to what is on the balance sheet.

INEXACT, BUT GOOD

Valuation is not an exact science. Book value is an accounting number, influenced by tax laws and management. It is only valid for a brief period.

Fortunately, book value does not have to perfectly measure the underlying value of a company's assets to be an effective tool for selecting stocks. Rather, it works because at the end of the day, a profitable, well-managed ongoing concern is using its assets to make money. The desks, the machines, the patents, and even the website address are worth more than their face value because they can increase shareholder's net worth. A company worth owning should be worth more than its book value.

THE P/E MULTIPLE

Considered by some to be the gold standard, the price-to-earnings (P/E) multiple is the most popular and best known measure of valuation. This multiple ties the price of a stock to a company's earnings.

In mathematical terms, the P/E is:
Stock Price / Earnings per Share

---

[5] The costs from dissident shareholder groups would start even prior to the liquidation process. The lawsuits would start at the time the prospect of liquidation is raised. Bondholders and other lenders may also choose to file lawsuits if they fear not enough money will be raised during the liquidation process to pay off outstanding liabilities.

The P/E multiple states how many times annual profits an investor is willing to pay for a stock. For example, if a company generates annual profits of $1 per share and the stock is trading at a P/E of 10, investors are willing to pay 10 times the earnings to own the stock. In other words, investors think the company is worth ten years of profits. Under this scenario, investors are considered to have full access to profits. If the company pays all of its earnings as dividends, 10 years from now, investors will receive their entire investment back.

This is a simplistic explanation, though. As discussed in chapters 5-7, a certain percentage of earnings needs to be reinvested in the business to pay bills, fund growth, and replace equipment. In addition, non-cash charges, such as depreciation, mask the amount of cash generated by the firm. On the flip side, profits from sales may be recorded before customers pay their bills.

As is the case with P/B, the P/E multiple or any other valuation measure is never perfect. But the P/E multiple does provide a useful tool for determining a stock's worth. A low P/E can signal that investors are apathetic toward a company or investors do not view the future prospects as favorable. A high P/E multiple indicates optimism for strong future growth is high. Over time, buying stocks at low P/E multiples results in higher returns than buying stocks trading with high P/E multiples. Multiple studies prove this and a dissection of the P/E provides the explanation of why.

EARNINGS YIELD

Earnings yield is a concept credited to Benjamin Graham. It is a means of calculating the rate of return implied by a stock's price.

Calculating earnings yield is easy; reverse the P/E multiple:
E/P = Earnings Yield

For instance, say a stock sells at $15 and with annual earnings of $1. We can quickly calculate the P/E multiple:

(P) Price = $15
(E) Earnings = $1
P/E = $15 / $1 = 15

Based on this information we can also calculate the earnings yield:

(E) Earnings = $1
(P) Price = $15
E/P = $1 / $15 = 6.67%

Buying a stock trading at a P/E multiple of 15 equals a yield of 6.7%. Unlike a bond, you won't receive an interest check every year equivalent to 6.7% of your investment. Instead, this is the implied return on your investment as measured by the current price and earnings. "Measured" is the key word. The stock may not generate a 6.7% return over the next year—it could appreciate more or decline in value. Rather, the earnings yield provides information as to whether a stock is attractive at its current valuation. Higher yields are more attractive than lower yields.

In traditional terms, yield is calculated from the price of a bond and its interest rate. A bond selling at face value, typically quoted as 100 (but actually worth $1,000), and paying an interest rate of 5%, will have a yield of 5%. An investor purchasing this bond can only expect to receive a return of $50 (5% x $1,000) a year if he holds the bond until maturity. At maturity, he receives the par value of the bond, which in this case happens to equal the purchase price price[6] and the last interest payment. If the investor pays $900 for the bond, he will receive $50 in annual interest ("coupon") payments plus 11% in capital appreciation at maturity.[7] Because the interest payment of $50 is based on the bond being worth $1,000 and the investor only paid $900, he locked in a yield of 5.6% ($50 / $900 = 5.6%).

Bond prices are primarily influenced by interest rates and the confidence in a company's ability to pay its debts. The more attractive the interest rate and the more certainty investors have in a corporation's ability to pay its debts, the more likely they are to pay a premium for the bond. The less confidence investors have or the less attractive the interest rate, the greater the chance the bond will sell at a discount. In either case, there is some expectation of being reimbursed for the face value ("par") of the bond at maturity.

With stocks, there is no expectation of being reimbursed. A stock is bought and sold at prevailing prices, which have nothing to do with a stock's par value (often a

---

[6] A bond is a promissory note – a loan. The face value of the bond is the amount of the loan. Bonds are typically created in $1,000 increments with quotes of about $100. The minimum investment is often $5,000 or $10,000 or sets of 5 to 10 bonds.

[7] The investor paid below face value or "par" for the bond. At maturity, he will be entitled to the full value of the bond, which in this case is 11% higher ($100 / $9,000 = 11%).

penny, anyway). More importantly, a stock's price will experience considerably more fluctuation than a bond's price will. In the event of bankruptcy, shareholders can make claims on assets only after all the bondholder claims have been satisfied. For these reasons, stocks are riskier than bonds. Given this higher risk, it is only logical for investors to demand a better yield on stocks than on bonds.

Hence, the concept of earnings yield. If a stock has a yield similar to bonds, shareholders are not being reimbursed for the additional level of risk. A stock with a low earnings yield may rise sharply in the future, but it could also depreciate. In the world of investments, expected returns are based on the level of risk involved. The higher the level of risk, the higher the level of return investors should demand. Why? Because at lower returns, investors could buy government bonds and keep their money safe. Why take the chance of losing money if the cash can be secured for the same amount of return? However, if there is a chance to make more money, then taking the chance of losing money may be a worthwhile endeavor. Earnings yield provides insight into whether the risk of buying the stock is worthwhile.

A base rate for determining if a stock's earnings yield provides adequate compensation is the interest rate of the 10-year Treasury note—an extremely safe investment. If 10-year notes are yielding 5%, investors should seek stocks with earnings yields that are at least 60% higher or a P/E of about 12. A P/E of 12 is conservative when compared against long-term returns.

Over the long-term, stocks have generated annual returns 60% higher than the returns generated by corporate bonds. Compared to treasuries, the differential is even greater. This difference is the rate at which the financial markets are compensating investors for taking the additional risk of buying stocks instead of bonds. Adherents of earnings yield point out that the greater the differential, the more safety an investor receives against bad news. A discounted stock could decline in the future, but the magnitude of the decline is likely to be less than a stock trading at a premium valuation. This is because the discounted valuation reflects existing apathy and/or negative sentiment, whereas the premium valuation reflects optimism for good news in the future.

GROWTH AND RISK

Another use of the P/E is to value a stock according to its future growth prospects. According to this methodology, stocks with higher P/Es should grow more strongly, while stocks with lower P/Es should report slower levels of growth. Mathematically, this use of the P/E is:

$$P/E = [D1/E1] / (k-g)$$

Where:

D1 = expected dividend of the stock for next 12 months

E1 = expected earnings for next 12 months

k = required rate of return

g = projected growth rate

The next chapter provides a thorough discussion of risk rates and growth rates, so I will stick to simplistic examples here.

Assume the required rate of return is equal to the long-term return on stocks, which is about 10%. The growth rate is one sustainable over the long-term. We will assume the company is mature and will achieve earnings growth in excess of economic growth, say about 5%. Finally, annual earnings per share (EPS) are projected to be $1 for the next fiscal year, and the dividend should be 50% of profits, or 50 cents per share. Using these assumptions, we can calculate the stock's value:

$$
\begin{aligned}
P/E &= [D1/E1] / (k-g) \\
&= [0.50/\$1] / (10\% - 5\%) \\
&= 0.50 / 5\% \\
&= 10
\end{aligned}
$$

According to these calculations, if the stock is trading at a price below $10 (P/E of 10 x EPS of $1), it is underpriced. If the stock is trading above this level, it is too expensive. Keep in mind we made assumptions about the long-term earnings potential of this stock and any adjustment to this forecast will affect the valuation. For example, let's raise the rate of growth to 8% instead of 5%.

$$
\begin{aligned}
P/E &= [D1/E1] / (k-g) \\
&= [0.50/\$1] / (10\% - 8\%) \\
&= 0.50/2\% \\
&= 25
\end{aligned}
$$

The stock has a higher valuation because it is expected to record stronger growth. However, assuming faster growth also leads to greater risk. The slower growth stock has an earnings yield of 10%, but the faster growth stock has an earnings yield of just 4%. In other words, all things being equal, investors are giving up compensation in exchange for what they hope will be stronger growth. The higher valuation is more risky because investors are taking a bigger chance that the company will achieve its goals. Most earnings forecasts prove to be wrong so investors have to ask themselves if higher valuations are a chance worth taking.

In both cases, the required rate of return was not altered and it was matched to the long-term return of large-cap stocks. Just as important, we assumed a stable rate of growth. Changes to either, or both, would result in different valuations. Rationally, the required rate of return for stronger growth should be higher because of the uncertainty involved with predicting future earnings.

In the next chapter, I will present mathematical models for calculating both risk and required return rates. These models are similar to what brokerage analysts use to calculate target prices for stocks.

Before we move on, there is another consideration—what period of earnings should be used for calculating earnings? The most common period is the previous 12 months, or the last four quarters. This is the period reflected in most P/E multiples.[8] The inherent problem with this is the last 12 months may not be reflective of historic or future trends. In fact, the period could be an aberration. This is why it is important to understand the business model, industry trends, and economic conditions.

Historic trends, particularly over the past five to 10 years, can show a company's performance in various economic environments. In theory, a company should be attractively valued if it trades at a reasonable multiple of past earnings. This thinking allows for the possibility that earnings could decline from their current level. Investors looking at economically sensitive companies should consider how profits have fared during periods of recessions. However, for companies with strong growth trends, such an analysis may not be completely reliable. Its use is limited to checking if the current valuation seems reasonable given the rate of growth. For example, if a stock is currently trading at a low P/E multiple despite a sharp increase in earnings over the past few years, more research is needed. After all, the low P/E may be a sign the market

---

[8] P/E multiples can be described as trailing (current stock price divided by the sum of earnings for the last four quarters) or forward (current stock price divided by the sum of projected earnings for the next four quarters).

does not believe the growth is sustainable. Without a clear and compelling reason why the stock can maintain its higher level of profitability, the current valuation needs to be questioned.

Some investors prefer to use projected earnings or a variation of the P/E multiple, called the PEG. Future earnings are dependent on the quality of the forecast and are best used as a sanity check rather than a direct measure of valuation. In the next chapter, I'll show you why.

KEY CHAPTER POINTS

1. Price-to-book value (P/B) is the most profitable measure of valuation.
2. A profitable, well-managed company should not trade for a price equivalent to or less than its theoretical liquidation value.
3. Valuation is an inexact science and there is no magic number where a stock suddenly becomes attractive. Although a good goal is to buy two times below the book value, it makes sense to pay slightly more for a quality company.
4. The earnings yield can reveal if an investor is being compensated for the higher risk of buying shares of stock instead of bonds.

CHAPTER 9

How Professionals Create Price Targets

Have you wondered how brokerage analysts decide what price target to put on a stock? Though price-to-book and price-to-earnings multiples are taken into consideration, the most often used measure is "discounted cash flow" or "DCF."

DCF is a mathematical formula designed to evaluate a company's future cash flows. It is an iteration of the Dividend Discount Model or "DDM," which assumes all stocks are worth the present value of all future dividends. When companies paid large dividends, DDM made sense. But now many companies yield small dividends or no dividend, or return money to shareholders in the form of share repurchases. Therefore, the DCF model makes more sense.

The theory behind DCF is investors are paying for how much cash a company will generate in the future. For example, if you knew a company would generate $10 million in cash each year for the next five years, would you pay $50 million right now? The answer is no, because of the risk that cash flows could be less than $10 million a year. You would also want to be compensated for profits you would receive by investing $50 million today in a five-year treasury bond, guaranteed to pay you interest. Therefore, you would want to pay a price below $50 million.

How much lower? That is what DCF calculates. It determines how much cash flows are worth today, based on the perceived level of risk and Treasury bond ("risk-free") interest rates. It is a discounting mechanism; meaning it acknowledges a dollar in the future is worth less than a dollar today.

DCF is used so often because a business is worth what future cash flows will be. A company could have been profitable in the past, but if it loses money in the future, past performance does not mean much. Put another way, if you are going to buy a business, you want to know it can make money; otherwise, you could lose everything. Think about your house. Would you have bought it if you thought it would decline in value? Of course not, unless you got it at a price so far below market value you would still come out ahead, even if prices declined.

In theory, DCF is a great model. In reality, it is only as good as its inputs. Inputs have a large margin for error, but DCF can be useful to determine if a stock is under or overvalued. It is a good tool to have, as long as you understand how it works and its limitations. In this chapter, I will break down the components of DCF and show how to create your own price targets.

You do not have to be a math person to understand the formula. As long as you can add, subtract, multiply, and divide on a calculator, you can calculate the formula. The formula might seem scary if you are not used to working with mathematical equations, but I will show you how to use it.

Even if you never run a DCF calculation, you will know enough to determine whether to trust a brokerage analyst's price target.

THE COMPONENTS OF DCF

Discounted Future Cash flow is a mathematical formula expressed as:

$$PV = \Sigma \frac{FV}{(1 + i)^n}$$

The formula is present value = the sum of all future cash flows, discounted by return, adjusted for time. Here is a legend explaining the formula in simplified terms:

PV – Present Value. The amount you are willing to pay today for future cash flows.

Σ – Sigma. When used in mathematical formulas, this Greek letter stands for the sum of all calculations. It is used to calculate how much all future cash flows are worth, not just those for the next one or two years.

FV – Future Value. Cash flow the company will generate each year in the future. You want to determine how much you would pay now for each dollar in the future.

i – Interest or Rate of Return. The percentage you want to earn on invested money. For example, you might be okay with earning a low rate on your bank savings account, because you know the money is safe. But if there is a risk of losing some of your money, you want a higher rate of return.

p. 149

n – Period of Time. How many years in which cash flows will be realized. For example, if you were calculating the present value of cash flows generated five years from now, you would use the number "5" instead of n.

Like any mathematical formula, DCF only works as well as the numbers that are used in it. Unfortunately, even small differences in "FV" and "i" can significantly change the stock's estimated value. Therefore, the first step in calculating DCF is to determine what inputs to use.

CASH FLOWS

The top half of the equation, FV, is the cash flows you expect the company to generate. Cash flows are defined as the amount of money eligible to be returned to shareholders; cash from operating activities minus capital expenditures. Cash flow is money generated by the company that does not need to be invested back into the business. For instance, consider a company like Ball Corporation (BLL), which makes cans and other packing products. For each can produced, the company needs to buy raw materials to make additional cans. It also needs to spend money on maintaining and, sometimes, replacing

model: what does a comp need to buy (raw materials)

machines. Therefore, not all profits realized by selling the cans are available to be returned to shareholders[1].

To determine what cash flows are, subtraction is required:

Cash from Operating Activities (found on the Cash Flow Statement)
- Capital Expenditures (found on the Cash Flow Statement)

= Cash Flow

This is a simplified method of determining cash flow, but it is a good estimate.

It is not uncommon for brokerage analysts to calculate cash flows for a company's separate divisions and combine them into a single number. Doing so can reveal trouble areas for the company and aids with forecasting future cash flows. If you want to calculate cash flows for each division, you need a spreadsheet and the patience to read through the company's SEC filings. A call to the company's CFO may also be required to clarify details. None of this is impossible, but the effort needs to be weighed against the benefit you will receive from doing so.

In the majority of cases, using the simplified model is sufficient to determine if a company is over or undervalued. Also the margin of error involved with forecasting future cash flows and risk rates is greater than the difference of using the simplified versus the complex method of calculating cash flows.

What about EBITDA?

EBITDA (Earnings Before Interest, Taxes, Depreciation, and Amortization) are often used as a substitute for cash flow. I prefer to use the aforementioned cash flow model instead. However, if you want to use EBITDA, subtract capital expenditures and add an increase or subtract a decrease in working capital.

You can use EBITDA as a substitute for cash flows when conducting a valuation analysis, but understand it will give you a broad valuation. If the share

---

[1] Cash flows are not profits. Profits are an accounting number calculated by taking the sales price and subtracting all the costs involved in producing, marketing, and selling a product, such as salaries, marketing, raw materials, and non-cash costs (e.g., depreciation). Cash flow is money received when the customer pays for a product. A portion of this needs to be reinvested into the business to maintain current operations and fund future growth.

Consider your paycheck. Your salary is different than your take home pay. You have various expenses deducted from your paycheck, such as taxes and insurance. As a result, the amount actually deposited in your bank account ("cash flow") is different than the total salary your company pays you ("profit").

price is significantly under this number, it is undervalued. Do not use EBITDA as your only means for determining a stock's valuation.

FV – Future Value

The numerator (top input) on the DCF model is a prediction. By assigning a value, you are saying the company's cash flow will change by X%. But how do you know what the actual cash flows will be?

Determine the numerator by forecasting cash from operating activities and subtracting future capital expenditures. I will explain how analysts forecast these numbers and show how to create your own projections.

FORECASTING CHANGES IN CASH FROM OPERATING ACTIVITIES

There are three parts of cash from operating activities that analysts emphasize when making projections: earnings, depreciation, and interest expense.

Earnings

Net income is the first component and the primary driver of future cash flows. Therefore, the accuracy of the forecast is the most significant factor in projecting cash flows. To create earnings estimates, brokerage analysts rely on a variety of resources: speaking to corporate executives, key customers, and suppliers; reading trade magazines; talking to economists; and using mathematical models to indicate possibilities. They also ponder a company's prospects because that is what they are paid to do.

Depreciation and Amortization

Brokerage analysts will divide a company into separate parts to determine the depreciation and amortization charges. These expenses are dependent on how much money has been and will likely be spent on capital expenditures and acquisitions.

I will discuss capital expenditures shortly. Forecasting acquisitions is more difficult, but an analyst considers industry trends and steps a company needs to take to maintain growth and market share.

Changes in Interest Expense

There are two parts for consideration: how much debt the company takes on and the interest on that debt.

The amount of future loans will be partially determined by capital expenditures. If investment in fixed assets increases, so will debt. What is more difficult to judge is if the company will take out new debt to acquire another firm, buy back stock or use it for some other purpose, such as financing regular business operations. Reviewing past business cycles and past acquisition history provides some insight. It is not uncommon for an analyst to calculate the financial implications of various scenarios to determine future debt.

To a certain extent, a company's interest expense will rise or fall according to the amount of outstanding debt. The variable is the finance rate of the debt, determined by the interest rate environment and future business conditions. An analyst will contact his firm's economists for predictions about interest rates. He will make adjustments based on how well the company is expected to perform.

Other Components of Cash from Operating Activities

Depending on the complexity of the spreadsheet and mathematical model, an analyst may consider other variables, such as changes in inventory levels. These will be based on assumptions about the business cycle and the company's spending patterns during similar cycles.

Once assumptions are made, the analyst will calculate future cash from operating activities. This is done by using the earnings projection and adjusting it by depreciation, amortization, interest, changes in working capital, and any changes in non-cash expenses.

CREATING YOUR OWN CASH FROM OPERATING ACTIVITIES FORECAST

With minimal effort, you can create your projection for cash from operating activities.

First you need a forecast for future earnings. Such forecasts are accessible on many websites. Concensus earnings estimates are the average of all forecasts made by brokerage analysts. The advantage is you are not reliant on the accuracy of one person; instead you benefit from all the analyses made by those paid to cover the company.

Earnings estimates posted on financial websites are projections for the current and next fiscal years, followed by a long-term growth rate. Depending on the brokerage firm, this long-term growth rate can vary from five to seven years. Therefore, to determine profits for years three, four, five, etc., apply the long-term growth rate to the second year's estimates.

For instance, if the company's forecast is to earn $1 per share in 2011 and the long-term growth rate is 10%, you can assume that 2012's profits will be $1.10 per share, or 10% higher. (The math is $1 x (1 + 10%).)

After calculating future earnings per share, you need to create a net income forecast. This is easy to do; take the earnings estimate for each year and multiply it by the number of shares outstanding for the most current period[2].

To adjust the net income number to cash flow, determine the historical averages of all line items for cash from operating activities. Here are the steps:

1. For each of the past five years, divide each line item (e.g., depreciation and amortization) by net revenues for that year. This will give you a historical average.

2. For the most current year, determine what each line item would have been had it matched the historical average. For example, say depreciation and amortization costs have averaged 10% of revenues a year. In 2009, the company generated $10 billion in revenues and reported depreciation and amortization expenses of $1.2 billion. Because the historical average is 10%, adjust the depreciation and amortization figure. The "normalized" expense would be $1 billion, which is 10% of the $10 billion in revenues earned. You make the same adjustment for every line item on the cash flow statement.

3. Using the forecast growth rate for earnings, based on consensus earnings estimates, calculate how much each cash flow line item will increase. For example, if earnings are projected to grow at a 15% pace next year, you would increase depreciation and amortization by 15% as well. (If you had revenue forecasts, you could use that instead for forecasting line items, but such projections are more difficult for individual investors to find.)

This calculation gives you a broad estimate, not an accurate forecast. Business conditions can and will change, but this calculation will give you a good enough number to determine future cash flows. Remember, you are trying to determine if a stock is over or undervalued, not what its exact trading price should be today.

---

[2] The number of shares outstanding can change due to share repurchase programs, secondary offerings, the issuance of convertible debt, and other factors. The possibility of dilution should be included in the earnings estimates, but there is a risk the assumptions used are incorrect.

CHANGES IN CAPITAL EXPENDITURES

Once cash flows from operating activities are forecast, they need to be adjusted for capital expenditures because the only cash available to shareholders is what is not reinvested. Subtract capital expenditures (CapEx) from cash flows from operating activities.

Forecasting capital expenditures requires assumptions about the company's growth and what it needs to match that growth; this involves dividing a company into parts and making economic and corporate forecasts.

Use General Electric (GE) as an example. Demand for its healthcare equipment should be stable, baring competitive threats. Calculating what capital expenditures have averaged relative to revenues can provide an estimate of future CapEx spending. The jet engine business, though, is dependent on economic conditions. When the airline industry is doing well, demand for jet engines increase, raising capital expenditure costs. When the airline industry is in a slump, overall spending decreases. As a percentage of revenues, spending on capital expenditures could increase. Therefore, knowledge about how GE adjusts its spending for each business unit, an understanding of each industry's business cycle, and the ability to forecast economic trends is required.

Commodity-related companies can be more difficult. An oil company will spend more on equipment and expansion when oil is above a certain price. When oil falls below a certain price, companies reduce spending. There is often a lull because CFOs want oil to maintain a certain price before aggressively spending. Therefore, to forecast capital expenditures, you have to make assumptions about not only where oil will trade, but how long it can maintain that price.

Brokerage analysts have an advantage; they have peers specializing in other industries providing insight. Most brokerage firms have economists who predict future growth and contraction. Analysts also have access to historical models and past spending patterns with changes in business and economic environments. Finally, they understand the companies they follow—and have time to determine the complex assumptions.

What is an individual investor, like you, to do? Create an estimate of future capital expenditures. From the cash flow statement, you can see the capital expenditures. Using the same process as for creating a historical average of cash from operating activities, calculate the historical percentage of revenues spent on capital expenditures. Then use this "normalized" number to forecast future capital expenditures based on forecast earnings growth.

If you think economic and business conditions will be better or worse in the future, look at how capital expenditures varied during a certain period. For instance, if capital expenditures rose significantly during periods of strong economic growth, increase your forecast for capital expenditures to match the same percentage of revenues as during the last period of strong growth. Similarly, if you think business conditions will worsen, decrease your forecast for capital expenditures. (If you have separate figures for depreciation and amortization, adjust only depreciation, in accordance with your CapEx forecasts.)

YOUR CASH FLOW ESTIMATE

Once you calculate cash flows from operating activities and capital expenditures, the math gets easy; subtract capital expenditures from cash from operating activities number for each year. This is your numerator.

THE PROBLEMS WITH FORECASTS

In showing how to calculate your own forecasts, I used the term "good enough." Though that may not inspire confidence at first glance, realize all forecasts are nothing more than educated guesses.

   Forecast Cash from Operating Activities
- Forecast Capital Expenditures

   Cash Flow Estimate

It would seem logical—given all their resources—that brokerage analysts would do well at predicting future earnings. Unfortunately they do not. Brokerage analysts often display a herd mentality. Profit forecasts do not vary much from analyst to analyst. Though there may be a difference between the highest and the lowest forecast, most profit projections are fairly close.

There are two reasons for this.

First, analysts are looking at the same data. Particularly in the age of fair disclosure and digital information, it is difficult to find information competitors will not have access to. At best, an analyst might have a few unique contacts, but these contacts add to the broader picture instead of providing a key piece of information that justifies a different forecast.

Second, if an analyst creates a forecast different from his peers, he will be questioned. If the analyst feels confident that he is seeing trends his peers are overlooking, he may accept the tough questions. More often, it is easier to create a forecast in line with what others are doing.

This does not mean you should not trust analysts' estimates. Quite the contrary. They are as close to an educated guess as you can get. But accept them for what they are—educated guesses.

The farther earnings are projected, the bigger the guess becomes.

Consider what happens with a game of roulette. On any given spin, the odds of the ball landing on a black or a red number are about 47%. The odds do not change with each spin. If a ball lands on a black number 10 consecutive times, the odds of it landing on a black number for an 11th time do not change; they remain at a 47% chance of landing on a black number and a 47% chance landing on a red number.

What does change is the compounding of losses, should you guess wrong and keep guessing wrong. Assume you bet red and the ball keeps landing on black. To win back your money, you start doubling the amount you bet. Here is what would happen after five spins:

You may have been confident in predicting what color the ball would land on, but each time you were wrong, a larger bet was required to offset your cumulative loss. The odds of roulette do not change, regardless of how many times a ball lands on red or black. This game offers a good example of how an

Spin	Bet	Loss	Cumulative Loss
1	$5	$5	$5
2	$5	$5	$10
3	$10	$10	$20
4	$20	$20	$40
5	$40	$40	$80

Chart reproduced with the permission of QuoteMedia. ©2010 Quotemedia.

incorrect forecast can turn against you.

Even if you make the correct forecast in the present, the future is rarely what you expect.

Imagine calculating the future value of Bear Stearns in January 2006. The latest information at that time would have shown it earned $1.46 billion. After analyzing the company's financial statements and business model, you assume Bear Stearns will stay profitable. You plug your forecasts into a DCF model and determine a price for the company.

A little more than two years later, J.P. Morgan (JPM) offered to acquire Bear Stearns for $2 per share—a substantial discount to any reasonable value the DCF model would have generated in January 2006. Even though the actual price paid by JPM was higher than $2, it was still below any price calculated, given what was known at the time.

The errors can work in the other direction as well.

Throughout 2008, the ability of Palm, Inc. (PALM) to stay in business was questioned. The company's products were out-of-date, management had lost credibility with investors, and there was uncertainty about the development

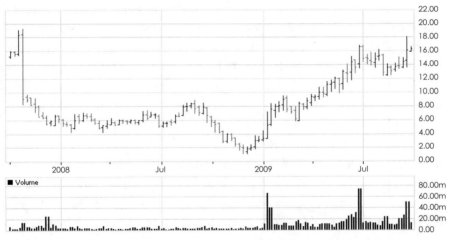

The introduction of a new product changed the outlook for Palm. Chart reproduced with permission of QuoteMedia. ©2010 Quotemedia.

of the new mobile phone operating system, much less whether it would pose a competitive threat.

In January 2009, the company unveiled a demo of a new phone, the Pre, at the Consumer Electronics Show. The presentation generated a lot of excitement and caused some investors to speculate about the company's profitability. Though the risks remained high, the outlook for Palm was brighter at the end of the January than at the beginning of the month. Hence, the stock prise rose.

There are also random, but significant events impacting a forecast.

Imagine calculating a value for Continental Airlines (CAL) or Delta Airlines (DAL) on August 31, 2001. Because of the September 11 terrorist attacks, the forecast would have been invalidated in less than two weeks.

Granted, these are extreme examples. As of this writing in fall 2009, Palm continues to have significant financial problems. However, these examples show how quickly forecasts can be wrong. (Palm was acquired by Hewlett-Packard (HPQ) in the summer of 2010.)

It is important to realize the factors invalidating a profit forecast do not have to be significant in determining if a company keeps its doors open. Apple (AAPL) altered the outlook for Nokia (NOK), Motorola (MOT), and other phone manufacturers when it introduced the iPhone in 2007. It was just one product, but it has influenced how smart phones are designed and how people interact with their phones.

Alternatively, the change can be gradual, but significant. Newspapers misunderstood the commercial potential of the Internet in the late 1990s. A 10-year profit forecast made in 1999 would not have accurately predicted the loss of advertising revenues to eBay (EBAY) or Monster (MWW), much less the threats that Google (GOOG) and craigslist have provided. None of this factors the drop in circulation. Yet the change in the technological landscape invalidated a forecast made in 1999.

A shift in the competitive landscape is the most probable event invalidating a long-term forecast. It may be the introduction of a new product, a change in technology, a merger creating a stronger rival or an unknown company taking market share. It slso could simply be that management missed a major opportunity to ensure growth. Whatever the reason, it is difficult to predict future profits.

Of course, the future is unpredictable. So why am I talking about it? Because a small change in a profit forecast can have a big impact on the value calculated by the DCF model. But the goal of DCF is not to give an exact value of a stock's worth, but to indicate a stock's valuation relative to its future expectations. Investors should be willing to accept uncertainty and a margin of error in their calculations.

If you are concerned about the margin of error, you can create several forecasts and apply probabilities to each. Alternatively, you could look at trends in earnings estimates. If estimates are rising for this year and next, you could use a slightly more optimistic forecast. Alternatively, if estimates are falling, you could use a more pessimistic forecast. A better option would be to ignore the forecast, but understand the value calculated by the DCF might be too low (if estimates are rising) or too high (if estimates are falling).

I – INTEREST OR RATE OF RETURN

The bottom half of the DCF equation is the rate of return you want on your investment. You want the return to be high as possible, but in reality, using a high number, say 50%, would make most stocks overvalued except in the worst market conditions[3]. What you need is a number providing adequate compensation for the risk of holding the stock.

The number you need is commonly referred to as the "risk rate." It is an adjusted return that, if achieved, justifies owning the stock. This number indicates if the stock has a chance of rising by X%, then it is worth the risk that future cash flows may be different than what you expect.

Going back to the example at the start of this chapter: if a company is projected to generate $10 million in cash per year for the next five years, how much would you pay? It would be less than $50 million, because there is the potential for cash flows to be less than $10 million per year. Therefore, you want to pay a discounted price for those cash flows. This discount is determined by the risk rate. How much of a discount do you need?

A commonly used method of calculating an appropriate risk rate is the Capital Asset Pricing Model (CAPM), which factors in the return you could earn by following a conservative investing strategy and the risk you take by investing in a stock. The model is designed to provide you with a risk-adjusted rate of return. The more a stock fluctuates in price, the higher the discount rate. In other words, more risk, more reward; less risk, less reward.

The model is:

$$R_s = R_f + \beta(R_m - R_f)$$

---

[3] Higher rates of return cause DCF to calculate a lower valuation because the formula assumes future growth will be stronger if a higher rate of return is used. For example, if you wanted to have $1,000 a year from now, you could invest $952 at a 5% interest rate or $910 at a 10% interest rate. At the end of one year, you end up $1,000 with either investment choice. The only difference is how much cash you need today. DCF works the same way; it calculates how much cash you need to invest today given a level of forecast cash flows and a specified rate of return. The higher the rate of return used in the formula, the lower the price you should pay for the stock today.

You may also see it as:

$$K_s = K_f + \beta(K_m - K_f)$$

Either way, it is the same formula. If you are intimidated by math, all you need to do is subtract, multiply, and add. You can run this formula with a calculator or a pen and paper. It is much easier than it looks.

The inputs are:

R_s – The required return for the stock

R_f – The risk-free rate; treasury bond rates are commonly used here

β - Beta, a number that calculates the volatility of a stock relative to the market

R_m – The market return rate or the return you could earn by tracking a major market index

R_f - Risk-Free Rate

The risk-free rate is the return you get by placing your money in a safe investment; one where you have virtually no chance of losing your investment dollars. Treasury bond rates are commonly used as the risk-free rate because the U.S. government has never defaulted on its debt. The rationale for this number is you always have the option of putting your money into a low-risk investment. Because of this option, you want a return in excess of Treasury bond yields to compensate for the possibility of losing money.

The 10-year Treasury bond rate is most commonly used for calculating the risk-free rate. Analysts often rely on projected bond rates provided by their firm's economists. Another practice is using the average bond yield for the past 12 months. Historically, long-term government bonds provided about a 5% return. This number would also work well, except for periods of extraordinary low or high interest rates.

R_m - Market Return Rate

You also have the option of investing in a mutual fund or an ETF that tracks an index, such as the S&P 500. The difference between the performance of investing in the broad index and treasury bonds is the market risk you incur by investing in stocks. This is also known as "systematic risk." If the market falls, so will most stocks. If the market rises, so will most stocks. Historically, investors have asked for an approximate 500 basis-point premium, or a total return of 10%, for investing in stocks over bonds.

Analysts have the luxury of accessing projected market returns from their firms. Most brokerage firms employ strategists who can provide a long-term outlook for stocks. But because you may not have this luxury, the conservative route is to assume, in any given year, the markets will generate a return of about 10%. This is close to the historical average. During times of strong economic expansion or contraction, the return may need to be adjusted, but in most instances, a presumed 10% market return will work.

β - Beta

Some stocks will experience bigger price swings than the market and some will fluctuate less. To adjust for this, beta is included in the formula. Beta is a mathematical measure of a stock's volatility relative to the broader market, most commonly, the S&P 500. A beta of 1.0 signifies a stock has experienced the same amount of price movement as the S&P 500. This does not mean the stock moves in the same direction as the S&P 500, but rather its price fluctuates with the same intensity. The stock is no more or less volatile than the broad market index.

A beta in excess of 1.0, say 1.5, means the stock is more volatile than the S&P 500. Such stocks are more likely to see big gains and big losses. Including beta in CAPM raises the risk rate for these stocks. A beta below 1.0, say 0.5, means the stock is less volatile than the S&P 500. It is less likely to experience a big upward or downward move. Including beta lowers the risk rate for these stocks.

Beta for most stocks can be found on most financial websites.

CALCULATING CAPM

The calculation for CAPM is simple once you have your inputs. We will use the historical averages for the risk-free and the market return rates. We will also assume the stock is more volatile than the S&P 500 and therefore has a beta of 1.2. Here is how the math would work:

$$R_s = R_f + \beta(R_m - R_f)$$
$$R_s = 5\% + 1.2(10\% - 5\%)$$
$$R_s = 5\% + 1.2(5\%)$$
$$R_s = 5\% + 6\%$$
$$R_s = 11\%$$

According to CAPM, we would want an 11% return to compensate for investing in this stock.

CAPM DOES NOT ALWAYS WORK

Though CAPM is commonly used, it is the subject of criticism. Entire academic papers have been written criticizing CAPM. Alternative methods have also been developed, such as the Arbitrage Pricing Model, which some analysts use.

For individual investors, such as yourself, the biggest problem with CAPM is calculating the required rate of return for high-risk stocks. This is because the CAPM may produce a rate too low relative to the probability that you could lose money. Therefore, alternative methods are required.

Some analysts will use junk bond rates or consult venture capital rates. Another method is to adjust the risk rate calculated by CAPM by the probability of the future cash flows being realized. For instance, a biotech analyst may adjust the risk rate based on the possibility of a new drug being approved by the FDA. For example, if a key drug is in Phase II trials, the risk rate may be raised to 50%. Though this may sound high, a Phase II trial means the drug is starting to be tested on humans; there is a risk the drug may never make it to market.

How much a risk rate should be adjusted upward is a judgment call. A rule of thumb is if a key product is being sold (or about to be released), but the company's ability to achieve or maintain profitability is questionable, a risk rate equivalent to junk-bond rates might be suitable. If key products have yet to be released, a considerably higher risk rate is warranted.

DIFFERENT RISK RATES FOR THE SAME COMPANY

Another common practice is for analysts to calculate separate cash flows for each primary division of a company and create separate risk rates for each stream of cash flows. This is useful if one division is more stable or risky than the other. To do this, analysts will look at other companies operating within the same line of business and use their risk rates as a basis. This works well for conglomerates and industry leaders with separate lines of business.

Calculating DCF

Determining the inputs is the most difficult and most important part of using DCF. The calculation is easy to run, though you will need a calculator or spreadsheet to do the math. (Various models can be found by searching the web.)

Here is the Discounted Future Cash model again:

For the purpose of running the calculation, assume cash flows will be $10 million per year for the next five years. We will also assume CAPM gives us a risk rate of 10%. Based on this, our inputs are:

$$FV = \$10 \text{ million}$$
$$i = 10\%$$

$$PV = \Sigma \quad \frac{FV}{(1 + i)^n}$$

We now need to run the calculation for each year:

According to the DCF model, if you were offered the chance to buy a business expected to generate $10 million in cash flows during each of the next five years, you should only pay $37.9 million. Doing so would give you a 10% return.

Why $37.9 million, instead of $45 million, which is 10% less than $50 million? You want to be compensated for the time value of money. Take a look at the calculations again. In year 1, if you invested $9.09 million at a 10% rate of return, you would have $10 million at the end of the year. If you invested $8.26 million for two years at the same rate of return, you would also have $10 million. How is this possible? Compounding. Let us look at the math.

You start by investing $8.26 million. At the end of the first year, you earn

Year 1	=$10 mil / (1 + .10)^1	= $10 mil / (1.10)	= $9.09 mil
Year 2	= $10 mil / (1 + .10)^2	= $10 mil / (1.21)	= $8.26 mil
Year 3	= $10 mil / (1 + .10)^3	= $10 mil / (1.33)	= $7.51 mil
Year 4	= $10 mil / (1 + .10)^4	= $10 mil / (1.46)	= $6.83 mil
Year 5	= $10 mil / (1 + .10)^5	= $10 mil / (1.61)	= $6.21 mil
			= $37.91 mil

$826,000 in interest, bringing the value of your account to about $9.09 million. In year 2, you receive interest on the current value of your account—not the starting value, so you earn $909,000 in interest, or 10% of $9.09 million. The two interest payments—$826,000 and $909,000—increase the amount of your investment to $10 million. Remember, your goal is to receive $10 million in cash flows two years from now, not today. What DCF calculates is how much you should pay today assuming a certain level of risk.

The numbers get smaller and smaller the farther out cash flows are forecast because you receive the equivalent of more interest payments. The percentage return does not change, but the value of your account does. Each year you move closer to receiving the cash flows, the bigger the balance becomes and the larger your interest payments become.

Look at the table on page 155 again. The difference in the present value of the cash flows between year 4 and 5 is only $620,000 because the account balance starts at $6.21 million. Between year 1 and 2, there is an $830,000 difference. The larger the starting account balance, the bigger the interest payment. The same thing happens with your savings account, though on a smaller scale. As the size of your account's balance grows, so do interest payments. This is the power of compounding.

TERMINAL VALUE

You are not going to invest in a corporation with a lifespan of five years. You want one that will stay in business. Therefore, you need to account for the cash flows beyond year 5, or whatever your forecast period. In theory, you could forecast cash flows far into the future, but you would end up with small numbers in your calculations. A better method would be to calculate a terminal value.

Terminal value is the amount all future cash flows are worth at the time an investment is sold. In essence, you are saying, "If I receive $X, I would be willing to give up rights to cash flows beyond this point."

This calculation requires one more assumption—the company's long-term growth rate. For some companies, this requires creating terminal values for various products. An example would be a pharmaceutical company whose drug patents expire on specified dates. Oil companies can have various termination dates based on their reserves. For most other companies, the long-term growth rate becomes more an educated guess. A good rule of thumb is 5%, which implies profits will grow at a pace faster than the overall economy. It is optimistic, but it will also provide a more conservative terminal value.

In the case of a high-growth company, you want to forecast cash flows beyond five years before using a terminal value. If analysts are projecting a 5-year growth rate of 20% per year, you could gradually lower the growth rate to a single number for years 6-10 and use a 5% terminal growth rate after year 10. This would allow you to factor in the potential for sustained high growth; but understand companies rarely maintain this level of growth.

Calculating Terminal Value

The formula for calculating terminal value is:

$$FV_{n+1} / (R - G_s)$$

The inputs are:

FV_{n+1} – The last year that cash flows are forecast

R – The risk rate, or required rate of return

G_s – The forecast rate of growth in the future, also known as the "stable growth rate"

To run the calculation, we will use our existing example, but assume at the end of year 5, you sell the business. We will also assume you made the necessary changes to allow cash flows to increase at a 5% growth rate far into the future. Finally, we will assume a 10% rate of return.

There are two calculations that need to be done. The first is the cash flow for year 6. Assuming the business will grow at a 5% rate, you need to increase annual cash flows by 5%. The math is simple:

$$FV_{n+1} = \$10 \text{ mil} \times (1 + 5\%) = \$10 \text{ mil} \times 1.05 = \$10.5 \text{ mil}$$

The second calculation is for terminal value:

$$\text{Terminal value} = \$10.5 \text{ mil} / (10\% - 5\%) = \$10.5 \text{ mil} / (5\%)$$
$$= \$210 \text{ mil}$$

This formula says the total of all future cash flows will be $210 million.

Adding Terminal Value to DCF

You include terminal value in your DCF calculation by adding it to your projected cash flows for year 5. This allows the terminal value to be discounted to a present value and to account for the risk that cash flows may never be realized.

The math changes to:

Based on the DCF model, the company's future cash flows are worth $168.3 million today.

Year 1	= $10 mil / $(1 + .10)^1$	= $10 mil / (1.10)	= $9.09 mil
Year 2	= $10 mil / $(1 + .10)^2$	= $10 mil / (1.21)	= $8.26 mil
Year 3	= $10 mil / $(1 + .10)^3$	= $10 mil / (1.33)	= $7.51 mil
Year 4	= $10 mil / $(1 + .10)^4$	= $10 mil / (1.46)	= $6.83 mil
Year 5	= ($10 mil + $210 mil) / $(1 + .10)^5$	= ($10 mil + $210 mil) / (1.61)	= $136.6 mil
			= $168.3 mil

IS THE COMPANY A BUY?

The DCF model tells you how much to pay for future cash flows, but does not tell you what the company is worth, for two reasons. First, the company holds a certain amount of cash (including marketable securities) and likely more than it needs to fund daily business operations. Second, bondholders have a seniority claim to future cash flows. In other words, the loan obligations must be paid before cash can be paid to shareholders. Therefore, you need to calculate the equity value of the company, or the value of shareholder's equity[4].

The formula is:

DCF Value + Cash - Debt

Say the company has $30 million in cash and marketable securities and $60 million in long-term debt outstanding (including the portion payable over the next 12 months). The math would be:

$168.3 mil + $30 mil - $60 mil = $138.3 mil

---

[4] The formula used assumes long-term debt. However, if there are other obligations, such as preferred shares or minority interests, those amounts also need to be deducted from the DCF value.

The equity value of $138.3 million is the company's worth to all shareholders. You can compare the equity value directly to the current market capitalization of the company or divide it by the number of shares outstanding to create a per-share price target. Ideally, the stock should be trading at a price significantly below the price calculated by DCF, say 10% or more. This will provide you with a margin of error if one of the assumptions is wrong. Conversely, if the current price is significantly higher than what DCF suggests, the stock may be too expensive to justify owning it.

DCF is useful for creating a price target based on a company's potential cash flows, but it is only a gauge. Because of the number of assumptions used to calculate the formula, it cannot accurately tell you a stock's price. However, when used with other forms of analysis, the DCF model can help you determine a stock's Risk-Reward Ratio.

KEY CHAPTER POINTS

1. Discounted cash flow (DCF) model calculates how much a company's future cash flows are worth today. This is a useful figure because when you buy a stock, you are paying for how much cash the company will generate in the future.
2. Like any mathematical model, DCF is only as good as its inputs, and its inputs have a large margin for error.
3. Components of DCF are future cash flows, rate of return, and the period of time cash flows will be forecast into the future.
4. Cash flows are the amount of money available to be returned to shareholders, meaning cash from operating activities minus capital expenditures changes in working capital.
5. The accuracy of the earnings forecast is the most significant factor in projecting cash flows. However, profit projections are nothing more than educated guesses about the future. A small change in the forecasts will have a big impact on the value calculated by DCF.
6. The risk rate is the rate of return that compensates you for the risk of holding the stock. Higher risk rates should be applied to companies yet to achieve or have problems maintaining profitability.
7. In addition to calculating future cash flows, calculate the current value of what all cash flows are worth beyond the year you intend to sell the stock. This is the terminal value.

8. The goal of DCF is not to give you an exact value of a stock's worth, but to tell you if a stock is undervalued or overvalued relative to its projected future cash flows.

PART 4

Creating Your Own Luck:

A Step-by-Step Process for Using the Risk-Reward Ratio to Manage Your Investments

CHAPTER 10

Applying the Risk-Reward Ratio to Your Portfolio

I started this book by saying smart investors create their own luck. Then I discussed the aspects of portfolio management and stock analysis that will allow you to lower your risk and increase your potential for reward. You now know what is required to create a diversified portfolio, evaluate a business model, analyze a financial statement, and assess a stock's valuation.

In this final chapter, I will show you how to use all these elements to turn the Risk-Reward Ratio in your favor. I will discuss how to apply the concepts, give you recommendations on creating your own luck today, and provide you with a scorecard for a quick evaluation of a stock's Risk-Reward Ratio.

APPLYING CHAPTER CONCEPTS

Investment Ideas

As discussed in Chapter 2, there is an endless source of investment advice. Brokerage analysts, fund managers, websites, newsletters, message boards, and even friends can give you ideas. You should be open to such advice because you never know when a good stock pick will be revealed. However, be sure to conduct your own analysis before acting on any stock tip.

When conducting the analysis, keep in mind the source of the advice. For instance, brokerage analyst recommendations are not as powerful as they could or should be. A more effective use of brokerage research is the change in earnings estimates. A clear trend of rising earnings estimate revisions is a positive sign; falling estimates are a negative sign. Financial advisors can be helpful, but consider your needs before hiring one. The investment media is a great source for new ideas, but many of the ideas may not be suitable for you. The web also provides a lot of information, but understand the quality of that information varies greatly.

You can balance the desire to hear new ideas and the requirement for thorough analysis by writing down any stock tip you hear and then researching it. Doing so allows you to maximize the potential for luck, while limiting the risk of acting on bad advice.

Portfolio Management

Your net wealth is determined by the dollar value of all of your investments, including your brokerage account, 401K, employee stock options, and your house. Therefore, you should think of all your investments—regardless of account—as part of one large portfolio. The upside will not only lead to improved diversification and decision making, but potentially a lower tax bill.

The decisions you make should be dependent on your age, income, and financial needs. Someone young and healthy can allocate a greater percentage of his or her portfolio to stocks than a retiree encountering medical issues. At the same time, you also need to consider the diversification of your portfolio. Regardless of age, health or wealth, your goal should always be to have a portfolio resting along the Efficient Market Frontier, which means using a mix of investments that are not directly correlated. Doing so can lower your portfolio's risk level while increasing the opportunity for reward.

Periodically review all the fees you pay for managing your portfolio (whether brokerage fees or mutual fund expenses) and determine if they are justified. Although every dollar in fees you pay is a dollar you will not see again, the value you receive for spending extra money may offset the cost.

Consider using a passive investment strategy to lower your transaction costs. Including passive investments can limit your downside risk by ensuring part of your portfolio is always tied to the performance of a major market index, such as the S&P 500. Furthermore, combining a passive investing strategy with an active investing strategy gives your portfolio an insurance policy while allowing you to go after bigger returns by selecting individual stocks and investments.

Psychology, Social Investing and Sentiment

The other key part of portfolio management is how you invest.

Every investment is a business deal—a means to make money—and emotions should not interfere with the decision to buy or sell a stock. This is easier said than done and why I recommend a written journal of all your investments. Write down why you bought a certain stock and what would cause you to sell it.

There are several reasons to sell a stock that, if followed, can protect you from taking a large loss on this stock. Price limits, including the 10-20 rule, selling half on a double, and trailing stops, remove the emotional component from investing decisions. Negative revisions to earnings estimates are another powerful signal to sell. Valuation and news can also determine the time to sell.

Most importantly, sell any investment keeping you up at night. You will be happier if you always follow this rule.

Technical analysis may help avoid investments keeping you up at night as well. A chart will show you how volatile a stock has been historically, whether a move in price has occurred, and what current sentiment suggests about the stock's risk level.

Also realize there is a monetary and opportunity cost to social investing. An economist will advise you to consider maximizing your profit opportunities to allow you to support your personal causes over the long-term. On the other hand, there are also moral and spiritual costs that need to be weighed. You need to find the mixture best for you.

Business Models

When evaluating a stock, one of the questions you should ask is "Do I know how the company makes money?" If not, do not buy the stock. Not only will you be unable to determine the trends helping the company, but you will also be unable to identify negative trends.

The key to a successful business model is a line of products that fulfills needs and is profitable. Conversely, companies fail because they cannot achieve sustainable profitability, do not adequately respond to change or fail to maintain customer loyalty. Barriers to entry should exist; without them, a company is unlikely to maintain good profit margins. Successful business models will help you make money; failing business models will cost you money. Remember that a company does not have to be an industry leader to be successful.

The Balance Sheet

Though the balance sheet is a snapshot of a company's fiscal status for one specific day, it can tell you if a company is adequately financed or has too much debt. The current, quick, debt/equity, receivables turnover, and inventory turnover ratios can make this determination.

As a rule of thumb, you want to invest in companies with a lot of cash and equity. Keep in mind the amount of cash, inventory, fixed assets, intangible assets, and debt will vary based on the industry in which the company operates. Companies that produce physical assets, such as manufacturers and fabricators, will have higher inventory, fixed assets, and liabilities than companies that provide more intangible assets, such as software or consulting services. Therefore, it is best to compare a company's balance sheet against that of its peers and not companies operating in completely different industries.

The Income Statement

The income statement is the most analyzed piece of financial data because it is the scorecard of a company's performance.

Most investors look at the income statement to see if revenues and earnings are growing. Though both revenues and earnings should increase over time, the rate of growth needs to be considered. A high rate of growth can be difficult to manage and many companies fail miserably at it. (If the growth is being driven by one key product, risks are even greater.)

Earnings growth can be masked by stock repurchase programs. Therefore, always look at the change in net income instead of only the increase in earnings per share.

Besides looking at growth in revenues and earnings, determine whether gross and net margins are improving over time. A trend of narrowing margins is a warning sign unless the company has proven it can more than offset the lower margins through higher sales.

Return on equity (ROE) is another good tool for assessing a company's earnings power. It calculates the return management is generating from the shareholders' stake in the company. ROE varies by industry, so it is important to compare a company against its peers instead of a company in a different sector. Preferably you want to invest in a company with a higher ROE than its peers.

The Cash Flow Statement

The cash flow statement is a snapshot of a company's cash balance—whether it has increased or decreased—and a running scorecard of how much money is coming in and going out. This is useful because there is a difference between earnings and cash. Earnings is an accounting figure and the cash balance depends on how much a company spends and how much it brings in.

When analyzing a cash flow statement, look for information that indicates the business model is making money and managment is acting in the best interest of its shareholders. Cash flows from operating activities will be positive for most years if the business model works and the company is well managed. Dividends, if paid, should increase over time. Debt should be used to fund expansion or replace expensive equipment, not to keep the doors open. If a company consistently takes on more debt, be cautious if net income is not rising. Similarly, the issuance of new stock is reason for caution and investigation.

The Two Most Profitable Measures of Valuation

Determining a stock's worth is the single most important component of the Risk-Reward Ratio. Though valuation is not an exact science, if you buy a fundamentally sound company trading at low P/B and P/E multiples, you will significantly turn the Risk-Reward Ratio in your favor.

Though the price-to-earnings (P/E) multiple is most often used, the price-to-book (P/B) multiple can lead to better returns. The rationale is that a profitable, well-managed company should not trade at a price equivalent to or less than its theoretical liquidation value. The organizational structure, in-place equipment and machinery, brand names, and marketing strategies all add value beyond what the assets could be sold at if the company ceased operations.

The P/E multiple should not be ignored. A high P/E can signal that many investors are optimistic about the future, increasing the downside risk.

Conversely, a low P/E can signal investors are pessimistic or apathetic, increasing the potential reward should the company announce good news.

The P/E multiple can also reveal if you are compensated for the higher risk of buying stocks instead of bonds. By inverting the P/E multiple to E/P, you can calculate a stock's earnings yield. A stock is considered to be cheap if its earnings yield is below that of similar bond yields.

How low a multiple should you pay? My preference is for stocks trading at a P/B multiple of 2.0 or lower and at a P/E of 12 or lower. I accept a P/B of 3.0 and P/E of under 20 if the business is sound and has a history of good revenue and earning growth. P/B multiples above 4.0 and P/E multiples above 25 signal the stock is speculative, meaning the risks are significantly higher.

How Professionals Create Price Targets

Brokerage analysts most often use DCF to calculate a stock's price target. This mathematical model determines how a much a company's future cash flows are worth today. DCF is useful because when you buy a stock, you are paying for how much cash the company will generate in the future.

DCF relies on three components: future cash flows, rate or return, and the time period in which cash flows will be forecast. Like any mathematical model, DCF is only as good as its inputs. Inputs have a large margin of error. Therefore, DCF should not be used to determine a stock's worth, but whether a stock is undervalued or overvalued relative to its projected future cash flows.

Seek out stocks trading at discounts of 10% or more to their DCF-calculated value. Such a margin will reduce the risk that one or more of the assumptions in the model are wrong. Conversely, if the current stock price is above what DCF suggests, it may be too expensive to justify owning it.

HOW TO START CREATING YOUR OWN LUCK

The first step is to catalog the assets you currently own. My preference is to use a spiral notebook, but a sheet of paper, an online portfolio, or a software program will also work. Your goal is to write everything down. List all the stocks, funds, options, real estate, annuities, and other investments you own and the dollar amount of each. If you have an interest in a partnership, write it down. If you are an art collector, write it down. If you own gold, oil royalties or some other commodity, write it down. Do not forget to list any saving accounts or CDs.

Once you have written down all your investments, categorize them. Group all equity investments together—stocks, options, and stock-based exchange-traded funds (ETFs) and mutual funds. Group your fixed income investments together, both bonds and funds that invest primarily in bonds. Do the same for commodities and real estate (do not forget to list your house). If there are assets you cannot easily sell, such as partnership interests (or assets you would be significantly penalized for selling early, such as annuities), group them together. Finally, group any assets not fitting into the other categories such as collectibles.

Determine Your Financial Goals

The next step is to determine your financial goals. Why are you investing? Are you saving for retirement? Are you setting aside money for a child's college tuition? Are you looking to buy your first house? Do you aspire to be wealthier than you are today? Or are you looking to protect your portfolio from inflation?

Everyone has a reason. You may have several financial goals, ranging from buying a new car to paying for a wedding to retiring early. Whatever your goals, write them down, along with an estimate of the timeframe you envision for them.

Seek A Financial Advisor or Not?

At this point, you should start thinking about a financial advisor. If you think you have or are gaining control over your portfolio, you may not need or want an advisor. Conversely, if you think you are not moving toward your goals or have difficultly figuring out how to accomplish those goals, sit down with an advisor. The work you will have done so far—listing all your assets and financial goals—will result in a more productive conversation.

Review Your Portfolio

If you decide to maintain control over your investment decisions, start a portfolio review process. You should do this at regularly scheduled intervals, preferably monthly. (Also plan on daily scanning any stock holdings for news and/or large movements in prices.)

The review process is simple and involves a few steps:
1. Analyze each stock and fund for any reason causing you to sell it, including a change in earnings estimates, an excessive valuation or a change in business

conditions. Consult the notes in your investing journal. (If you have not kept an investing journal, now is the time to start. Write down why you bought each stock and what would cause you to sell them now. Also conduct a new analysis of each stock using the Risk-Reward Scorecard.)

2. Review the list of investments to ensure they are diversified. Flag any overlapping investments, such as holding IBM (IBM), Cisco Systems (CSCO), and a technology fund for further analysis. Make sure your portfolio is not too heavily weighted in a single stock, industry or sector.

3. Determine the broad asset classes of your investments and determine if the allocation is within the range required by your financial goals. Since the allocation percentages will shift from month to month, do not worry about a small change. Also keep an eye out for asset classes, such as commodities, that have risen from comprising 10% of your portfolio to 20%.

THE RISK-REWARD SCORECARD

Once you know your goals, what you own and what could cause you to sell your stocks, you can start looking for new stocks. Though I recommend a thorough analysis of a stock before buying it, the following scorecard will help assess a stock's Risk-Reward Ratio.

What is the P/B Multiple?

Answer	Score
Below 2.0	1
Between 2.0 and 3.0	2
Between 3.0 and 4.0	4
Above 4	5

NO 3's

What is the P/E Multiple?

Answer	Score
Below 12	1
Between 12 and 20	2
Between 20 and 25	4
Over 25	5

Is Cash from Operating Activities Positive?

Answer	Score
Yes for the last five years	1
Yes at least three (including the last reported fiscal year) of the last five years	2
No for at least three (including the last reported fiscal year) of the last five years	4
Not for most of the last 5 years	5

Are revenues, net income and EPS increasing?

Answer	Score
Yes for the last five years	1
Yes at least three (including the last reported fiscal year) of last five years	2
No for at least three (including the last reported fiscal year) of the last five years	4
Not for most of the last 5 years	5

Have earnings estimates risen or fallen over the last 30 and 60 days?

Answer	Score
Earnings estimates for this year and next have risen	1
Earnings estimates for this year and next are basically unchanged	3
Earnings estimates for this year and next have fallen	5

Does the company sell products that fulfill needs, is it profitable, and does it operate in a market with barriers to entry?

Answer	Score
Yes	1
Yes to 2 of the 3 characteristics	3
No	5

What is the company's current ratio?

Answer	Score
Above 1.0, but below 2.0	1
Above 2.0	3
Below 1.0	5

What is the company's debt/equity ratio?

Answer	Score
0.5 or lower	1
0.5 – 0.75	3
0.75 – 1.0	4
1.0 or higher	5

How does the company's ROE compare to its peers?

Answer	Score
Better than its peers	1
About the same as its peers	3
Worse than its peers	5

Does the stock add to your portfolio's diversification?

Answer	Score
Yes	1
No	5

Calculate a stock's Risk-Reward Ratio by rating it according to each of the 10 questions, using the scale previously listed and add total points for each stock.

Total Points

10-14 =	Very good; the Risk-Reward Ratio favors buying the stock
14-25 =	Good, the Risk-Reward Ratio favors buying the stock, though risks are higher
25-35 =	Average; the potential risks and rewards are about even
35-45 =	Bad; the Risk-Reward Ratio favors selling the stock despite potential for reward
45-50 =	Very bad; the Risk-Reward Ratio favors selling the stock

As you can see, lower scores suggest a lesser amount of risk and a greater amount of reward. The more you can get the Risk-Reward ratio in your favor, the better your opportunity for profit. Keep in mind the scoreboard does not factor in recent news events or the volatility displayed on a chart, so check both before making a final decision as to whether to buy or sell a stock.

CONCLUSION

I would love to tell you there are plenty of perfect stocks out there waiting to be bought. The reality is you will find few that score a perfect 10. There are many stocks whose potential rewards outweigh their risks (scores of 14-25). Such stocks may not be perfect, but they are capable of building wealth. As long as you focus on investing in stocks whose Risk-Reward profiles are favorable, you will create your own luck.

Glossary

10-K
An annual report required by the Securities & Exchange Commission that discusses a company's business model, risks, legal actions, and financial status

ACCOUNTS PAYABLE
Money a company owes to its vendors

ACCOUNTS RECEIVABLE
Money the owed to a company by its customers for products sold or services rendered

ACCRUED EXPENSES
Expenses that the company will have to pay within the next 12 months but are not due as of the date of the balance sheet

ACTIVE
A strategy where the investor or a money manager directly selects the securities to invest in

ADDITIONAL PAID-IN CAPITAL
The difference between the offer price of common stock and the par value of the shares

ALPHA
The proportion of a portfolio's return attributable to your, or a money manager's, stock picking abilities

AMORTIZATION
The deterioration in value of an intangible asset due to the passage of time This is a non-cash charge

BACKLOG
The amount of unfilled orders a company has

BARRIER TO ENTRY
Anything that dissuades a would-be competitor from entering the market for a product or service

BASIC SHARES
The total amount of shares outstanding as of the date of the income statement

BETA
A mathematical measure of how volatile a stock is relative to the broader market

BOOK-TO-BILL
A measure of future revenue streams. It is the amount of orders ("book") relative to the number of orders that can be shipped or "billed"

BROKERAGE ANALYST RECOMMENDATION
A stock rating published by a brokerage firm with the primary purpose of encouraging an investor to buy or sell a security, such as a stock

BUSINESS MODEL
What the company does to make money. It may manufacture, fabricate, develop, provide, distribute or sell various goods and services

BUY SIDE
Money managers, mutual funds and related financial professionals who are hired to invest money on the behalf of their clients and beneficiaries. The term refers to the fact that these professionals look for investments to invest in as opposed to making buy and sell recommendations

CAPITAL EXPENDITURES
Cash spent on fixed assets such as machinery, vehicles, buildings, furniture, fixtures, etc.

CAPITAL LEASE
A lease used to acquire machinery, a building or some other costly fixed asset

CASH FLOW NEGATIVE
A company is spending more cash more than it is bringing in

CASH FLOW POSITIVE
A company is bringing in more cash than it is spending

CONSENSUS EARNINGS ESTIMATE
This is the average of all profit forecasts made for a particular company

COST OF REVENUE
Also commonly called "Cost of Goods Sold", this is the amount a company spends manufacturing, fabricating or producing a product

CURRENT ASSETS
Assets that are highly liquid (e.g., cash) or are intended to be used within the course of the next 12 months

CURRENT RATIO
A measure of how liquid a company is, or, how able it is to meet its current obligations

CYCLICAL
A company whose growth rate is tied to the strength or weakness of the economy

DEBT/EQUITY
A ratio that reveals how leveraged a company is

DEFERRED CHARGES
An upfront expense that provides a benefit over a lengthy period of time. The company can spread the charge against several years of income, instead limiting it to the year the expense occurred

DEFERRED INCOME
Money received for a service or product that has yet to be delivered

DEFERRED INCOME TAX
A liability that arises when there is a difference between what the company reports to tax authorities and what it reports to shareholders

DEPRECIATION
A non-cash charge that accounts for the decrease in value of a fixed asset due to age and wear and tear

DILUTED SHARES
The total amount of shares that would be outstanding if all options, warrants, convertible bonds, and convertible preferred shares were turned into common stock

DISCOUNTED CASH FLOW (DCF)
A mathematical formula designed to calculate how much a company's future cash flows are worth

EARNINGS ESTIMATE
Also called the consensus earnings estimate, this is the average profit forecast published by brokerage analysts

EARNINGS SURPRISE
The amount by which a company exceeds (positive) or misses (negative) the consensus earnings estimate for a specific quarter

EBITDA OR EARNINGS BEFORE INTEREST, TAXES, DEPRECIATION, AND AMORTIZATION
A proxy for cash flow

EFFICIENT MARKET FRONTIER
Based on Harry Markowitz's Modern Portfolio Theory, it is the point at which a portfolio's diversification provides the maximum level of return relative to its inherent level of risk

FINANCIAL ADVISOR
A broad term that refers to a professional hired to help an investor manage his portfolio. A financial advisor can be a financial planner and stockbroker

FOREIGN EXCHANGE EFFECTS
An accounting entry designed to reconcile differences caused by the translation of cash flows generated in different currencies

FFO OR FUNDS FROM OPERATIONS
A measure of how much cash flow a trust, such as a REIT, is generating

GOODWILL
Any amount paid in excess of the underlying value of the net assets when an acquisition is made

GROSS MARGIN
The percentage profit a company makes on goods sold

GROSS PROFIT
The amount of money a company earns on all products sold or services provided within a certain period of time (e.g., a quarter or a year)

INSTITUTIONAL INVESTOR
Typically pension funds, endowments, insurance companies or money management firms, these are entities with a large amount of cash to invest

INTANGIBLES
Non-physical assets that a company believes has value

INTEREST COVERAGE RATIO
A ratio that calculates a company's ability to make its interest payments

INVENTORY
Any physical item related to the production or packaging of a product

INVENTORY TURNOVER
A measure of how quickly a company is going through its inventory

LOAD FACTOR
How much a plane's capacity is utilized by paying customers or cargo

LONG-TERM DEBT
Loans scheduled to be paid over a period in excess of 12 months

MINORITY INTEREST
A stake in a company or subsidiary that represents less than 50% ownership

MONEY MANAGER
A person or firm hired to invest money on the behalf of institutional or individual investors. Money managers directly manage portfolios as opposed to simply advising a client what securities to buy and sell

MOVING AVERAGE
A line that tracks the average price for a set period of time, such as 50 days. It is called a moving average because the line traces the average price for each day and moves up or down, depending on whether the average price is higher or lower

NET INCOME
The profits available to shareholders after all expenses and taxes are paid

NOTES PAYABLE
Short-term loans made to a company

NOTES RECEIVABLE
A loan or extension of credit

OPERATING INCOME
The total amount of money a company is making from its regular business operations

OPERATING MARGIN
Operating income divided by revenues

PASSIVE
A strategy where the portfolio is designed to mimic the construction and performance of an index

PREFERRED STOCK
A hybrid security that pays a regular dividend but does not offer any voting power

PREPAID EXPENSES
Expenses that are paid for in advance

PROPERTY, PLANT & EQUIPMENT
Also referred to as "fixed assets," these are the tangible assets required to run a business and are meant to last for more than a year

QUICK RATIO
A ratio that shows whether a company can meet its obligations if inventories are excluded from current assets

RATE OF RETURN
The percentage return sought in exchange for investing in a certain security

RECEIVABLES TURNOVER
A measure of how quickly company is paid by its customers

R&D OR RESEARCH & DEVELOPMENT
Expenditures for researching and developing new products and services (or improving existing ones)

RESISTANCE
A price level that a stock has had difficulty rising above. This can either be a new high for the stock price or the lower level of a previous higher trading range

RETAIL INVESTOR
An individual who invests in stocks, bonds, funds, or commodities is referred to as a retail investor. Very few individual investors have enough assets to be considered an institutional investor

RETAINED EARNINGS
Net income minus any dividends that have been paid

ROA OR RETURN ON ASSETS
How effectively management is using the firm's assets to generate income

ROE OR RETURN ON EQUITY
The return management is generating from the shareholders' stake in the company

REVENUES
Also called "sales," this is the money paid to a company for the provision of goods and services

RISK-FREE RATE
The return you would get by placing your money in a safe investment; one where you had virtually no chance of losing any of your investment dollars

RISK/REWARD RATIO
The amount of potential upside relative to the amount of potential downside

SAME-STORE SALES (AKA COMPARABLE STORE-SALES OR COMP STORE-SALES)
The change in revenues for store locations open for one or more years

SG&A OR SELLING, GENERAL, AND ADMINISTRATIVE EXPENSES
Overhead expenses, which can include marketing, human resources, rent, utilities, office supplies, legal fees, etc

SELL-SIDE ANALYST

A financial professional who makes buy and sell recommendations on stocks and other investments These individuals are hired by brokerage firms to attract clients and generate trading commissions

SHORT-TERM INVESTMENTS

Stocks, bonds and warrants that the company intends to sell over the next 12 months

SOCIAL INVESTING

Making investing decisions based on one's religious, spiritual or political beliefs

SUPPORT

A price level that a stock does not fall below for a period of time. This can either be a new low for the stock price or the upper level of a previous lower trading range

TECHNICAL ANALYSIS

A method of forecasting whether a stock is headed higher or lower based on historic price and volume trends

TERMINAL VALUE

The amount all future cash flows are worth at the time an investment is sold

TRACKING ERROR

The difference between the return of an index and a portfolio designed to mimic that index

TRAILING STOP

An order to sell a stock if it declines by a preset percentage or dollar amount; the actual price the sell is executed at adjusts higher if the stock continues to trend higher

TRANSACTION COSTS

Any expense incurred in the transfer of assets, such as brokerage commissions or mutual fund fees

TRANSACTION COSTS

This is any expense incurred while trying to buy or sell a security It includes commissions, brokerage fees, taxes, the difference between the bid and the ask price, and any change in the security's price caused by the transaction order

TREASURY STOCK

Shares purchased by a company

Index